Toddler Parenting

The Ultimate Guide to Using Positive Discipline to Raise Children with High Self-Esteem, Including Tips for Sleep Training, Handing Tantrums, and Potty Training

Contents

Introduction

Imagine a home with happy children who listen to their parents and don't misbehave. A home where no one must raise their voice, and everyone is happy. This book will give you all the information you need to turn this peaceful thought into reality. Raising a child isn't always easy, no matter how much love you have for your little one. No single approach would fit all children. Sometimes, you wish your toddler came with an instruction manual. Alas, this isn't the case.

Being a parent is perhaps one of the most memorable, dynamic, and exciting roles you will ever play. Parenting is rewarding and fruitful, but it can be difficult. Parents have no formal training before they are made responsible for dealing with kids. It can also be a little overwhelming and daunting. Even the best of us require some support. Well, you can rest easy because this book has all the information you need to understand about positive parenting to raise a well-adjusted, happy, and confident child.

In this book, you will learn about understanding your toddler's development, the meaning of positive discipline and its importance, and tips and suggestions to get started with positive parenting. You will also discover helpful and practical tips for potting training and sleep training for your toddler. Besides these things, you will learn about dealing with your toddler's tantrums, correcting any misbehavior, and helping your toddler form positive habits. When all the information in this book is implemented, it helps encourage your toddler's creativity and imagination and build self-esteem and confidence. Simple and practical tips for applying positive discipline once your toddler grows and enters the age of schooling are also included. This book includes all the information any parent would need to get started with positive parenting.

Once you follow the practical advice in this book, you will see a positive change in your toddler and the relationship you share. Taking care of children isn't just about looking after their basic needs of food, clothing, and shelter. An important aspect of parenthood and your duty as a parent is to equip your child with the skills he needs to survive in the real world. As with everything else, the sooner you start, the more effective and efficient are the results. A little love, patience, consistency, and effort are all you need to change your toddler's behavior.

Are you eager to learn more about all this? Do you want to discover the concepts of successfully parenting your toddler? If yes, let's get started without further ado!

Chapter One: What It Means To Be A Toddler

There are different terms used to describe children between the ages of birth to four years, such as infants, babies, newborns, and toddlers. These terms are often used synonymously, but there is a slight difference between each. Until the baby is two months old, he is called a newborn. The infant is a term used to refer to children until they are 12 months old. Baby is a term collectively used to refer to children who are or less than four years old. Therefore, it includes all the other terms, such as infants, toddlers, and newborns.

Who is a toddler? It turns out there isn't any official definition or an upper limit to the term toddler. Often, it's a term used to define children between the ages group of 12-36 months. The Centers use the same definition For Disease Control And Prevention. A toddler is a child who is learning to walk or toddles. This stage usually starts when a child is about 12 months old. The period between 12-36 months is critical for the baby's growth and development. There is a lot of change your baby needs to get accustomed to during this period. From learning new skills such as interacting with others or talking and walking, to becoming independent, this stage is all about growth.

Major Toddler Milestones

All the things that your little one can do will excite and surprise you. From the first step he takes to the words he utters and the real interactions through verbal and non-verbal communication, there is a lot to look forward to. There are critical milestones for every toddler, which determine his overall growth and progress. Usually, a baby takes his first steps around his first birthday, but this can also vary. No two individuals are alike, and the same stands true for toddlers too. The first milestone, you need to watch out for is when your baby learns to walk. This usually happens when the baby is between 12-18 months old. Parents often worry when their baby doesn't do things that other babies do. Don't be in a rush, and don't worry because they also grow at their own pace. As your baby grows, he will walk alone, run, and indulge in simple physical activities with objects such as playing with a ball or pulling his toys.

Between the ages of 10-14 months, babies utter their first words. Be a little patient, and you might need to listen to a lot of gibberish before he speaks real words. Even if your toddler isn't communicating using actual words, don't worry. Instead, look for other ways he's trying to communicate with you. Other forms of non-verbal communication include pointing, nodding his head, or even staring in a specific direction. It is also an age during which toddlers learn social and emotional skills that help them understand simple concepts such as making others laugh and associating names to their feelings and emotions.

Usually, here is the basic development; you might see your toddler when he is between 12-17 months old.

- Get attached to a stuffed toy or a blanket.
- Starts showing a preference for a specific hand (uses his dominant hand)
- Loves to play games
- Holds out his arms when you dress him
- Has probably perfected one or two simple words

- Understands the concept of a reflection he sees of himself in the mirror
  - Can bend and pick up objects
  - Can follow simple instructions
  - Starts eating with fingers
  - Points at objects
  - Tries to stand up from a sitting position
  - Grabs hold onto small objects.
  - Starts scribbling
  - Can chew bigger pieces of food
  - Understands and obeys instructions
  - Starts to run
  - Shows preferences specific foods
  - Tries to climb
  - Shows an affinity for specific colors

Here are the basic developmental milestones you might see your toddler when he is between 18-36 months old.

- Might understand instructions but does not necessarily follow them
  - Excitedly dances to music.
  - Starts insisting on eating by himself
  - Likes helping adults with their chores
  - Can identify body parts such as eyes, nose, and mouth
  - Stops putting different objects he picks up in his mouth
  - Starts reading on his own, even if it sounds like gibberish
  - Bedtime struggles start
  - Understands the difference between right and wrong
  - Can link two words together
  - Starts undressing on his own
  - Learns to throw a ball or other objects
  - Starts to walk up and down the stairs slowly
  - Has better communication skills
  - Can brush teeth by himself
  - Can identify objects or people in pictures

- Learns to understand the meaning of propositions
- Can show shyness
- Loves interactive games and stacking
- Wants a lot of attention
- Can identify his likes and dislikes
- Starts responding to basic questions and talks about himself

Common Toddler Troubles

Aggression

You might be worried when your toddler becomes aggressive and at his external displays of aggression through hitting or biting. As unpleasant as it sounds, it is common. It's often due to his desire to be independent. This, coupled with the fact that he cannot control his impulses and is just learning language skills, trigger his aggressive behavior. However, it doesn't mean all this is acceptable. You will learn more about dealing with undesirable behavior using positive parenting in the subsequent chapters.

Screaming

Some toddlers scream because they want attention, or they are denied something. Sometimes, toddlers shout to test their parents' boundaries. Screaming is your toddler's way of getting your attention, and it is something he desires.

Lying

Active imagination and forgetfulness are the two common reasons toddlers lie. Their inability to differentiate between reality and imagination can make it difficult for them to distinguish between what has or hasn't happened.

Tattling

It is believed toddlers often resort to tattling to get attention, increase their self-esteem, or display their power. It helps your child believes he has one-up another kid. He also wrongly believes that it makes him look more positive in the eyes of adults around him. They tattle because they haven't developed the emotional or social skills required to understand how to solve their problems.

Interrupting

Toddlers somehow believe the world revolves around them. Their short-term memory is still developing, and they strongly need to say things right away before they forget. This is one reason why they constantly interrupt others while talking. Also, the idea of interruptions does not exist in your toddler's head. Don't understand that others might want to say things or do things that are beyond their interest.

Throwing Tantrums

Another common problem during toddler years is tantrums. The toddler understands more verbal communication but is still not at a stage where he can freely communicate what he wants. This inability to communicate can make him feel helpless and results in tantrums.

Teasing

When your toddler is about two years old, he understands what boundaries mean, and he keeps testing them to understand where his limits are. Toddlers like teasing, but it's never with any malicious intentions. It is a sign of his cognitive development.

Whining

Your toddler depends on you for every basic need or desire, whether or not it is food or love - he relies on you. If he doesn't get your attention when he needs it, it becomes a challenge for him. This results in whining. The high pitch used during whining is his way of trying to get your attention when one of his needs hasn't been met.

Throwing Things

When a child is between 18-36 months old, he develops and fine-tunes his motor skills. A simple way he learns to do this is by picking up and throwing objects. Your toddler doesn't do this to irritate or annoy you. Instead, he thinks of it as an enjoyable activity and often does it to practice his motor skills.

None of these behaviors are desirable but are to be expected. You will learn more about fixing such behaviors and replacing them with desirable ones in the next chapters.

Chapter Two: What Is Positive Discipline?

Before learning about positive discipline, it's essential to understand the difference between discipline and punishment. These two terms are often used synonymously, but they couldn't be more different. Simply put, discipline involves positive methods that teach a child to be confident, responsible, and exert self-control. Instead of telling your child what he's not supposed to, it helps to teach him what is okay and what isn't okay. With discipline, you can teach your child new skills to regulate his behavior, problem-solving techniques, and deal with any unpleasantness. It enables him to learn from his mistakes and replace them with socially appropriate ways to handle himself. Instead of taking away his privileges, shouting or spanking, disciplining helps him avoid undesirable behaviors.

But punishment includes punitive measures. It essentially means you are giving your child a penalty for any misbehavior or offense. It's about making your child pay for his misbehaviors. At times, parents also punish their kids because they are frustrated. It can also stem from the desperation that the parent yells, spanks, or takes away a privilege given to his child. To send a message that his behavior needs to change or else he will be yelled, spanked, or his privileges will be taken away. The main problem with punishment is it doesn't teach good behavior. It might tell him he's not supposed to do something because he will be punished otherwise. He might feel confused about why it is okay for you as a parent to yell at him, but he is not supposed to do this.

Another major problem with punishment is it makes children feel out of control. When you teach appropriate behaviors and why certain behaviors are undesirable, it gives a better sense of control. It makes him feel like he in complete control of his actions and any natural consequences that follow either direct result of his actions.

Meaning of Positive Discipline

Dr. Jane Nelsen is accredited with creating the program of positive discipline. Her work relies heavily on the teachings of Alfred Adler and Rudolf Dreikurs. The idea behind positive discipline is to equip young people with the skills they need to become respectful, responsible, and resourceful members of the society. It helps teach quintessential life and social skills, which is respectful and encouraging for adults and children alike.

It is a natural human tendency to connect with others, and this desire is rather strong in children. Once your child feels this sense of connection to his family and others around him, chances are his misbehavior will reduce. Positive discipline is based on mutual respect, effective communication, problem-solving techniques, understanding the reasons for a specific behavior, encouragement, and concentrating on the solutions instead of the problem. Positive discipline teaches parents to be proactive instead of reactive. It's always easy to fix the situation before it worsens, instead of reacting to it when it's bad.

When you teach your child good behaviors and why certain behaviors are undesirable, exhibiting such behavior reduces. If you talk to him while he is calm and composed, he will be more likely to listen to you. If you try explaining all this to him when he's throwing a tantrum, it will merely worsen the situation.

Benefits of Positive Discipline

Positive discipline helps improve the bond between parents and children. It also strengthens the connection you share. If you continually punish your child, give him timeouts, take away his privileges, or shout at him, it strains the relationship. It can also create resentment in the kid. The tactics used for practicing positive discipline are mutually encouraging and respectful. You learn to be kind and firm to your child. Instead of punishing him, when you calmly explain why he's not supposed to do something, he probably will listen to you.

It is also effective in the long run. When your child knows what he's supposed to do and not supposed to, and the reasons for the same, it becomes easier to teach him good behaviors. When you punish him for any misbehavior, it merely illustrates that he isn't supposed to do something. However, it doesn't give him any skills or lessons essential for learning good behavior. Even if punishment works, the benefits it offers are only momentary.

Another advantage of positive discipline is it teaches children vital social and life skills such as respecting others, being considerate, learning to solve problems, and cooperating with others. All these skills will turn your child into an adult; you will respect, love unconditionally, and admire.

According to, "Relations Among Positive Parenting, Children Suffered Full Control, And Externalizing Problems: A Three-Wave Longitudinal Study," (2005) and "Intergenerational Continuity In Parenting Behavior: Mediating Partisan Child Effects" (2009) positive discipline helps foster emotional growth, but academic performance, improves mental health and provides better outcomes in terms of trials behavior.

Positive discipline also gives your child the chance to understand how capable he is. It helps build his self-esteem and confidence.

Principles of Positive Discipline

Positive discipline is a simple concept based on practicality. There are no standardized principles of positive discipline, but some ground rules need to be followed. In this section, let's look at the core principles of positive discipline.

Principle #1: Shift Focus

It is easy to say, "Don't do this," but it serves no purpose. Instead of harping on the things your toddler isn't supposed to do, positive discipline helps tell him what he can do. Instead of saying, "Don't run around the house," with positive discipline, you are taught to say, "Walk carefully instead of running." It also helps make the child understand why certain actions aren't desirable. If you catch your little one running carelessly, you can tell him, "If you run in the house, you can fall and hurt yourself." By explaining, it becomes easier to make him understand why certain behaviors aren't desirable.

Principle #2: The Child's Feelings

If your child makes a mistake or misbehaves, instead of getting upset with him and shouting or yelling, positive discipline teaches you to become more considerate about your child's feelings. No child is inherently bad. It is just the behavior that needs to be changed. If your child spills his food, don't say, "You are a bad boy!" Instead, you can concentrate on the action or behavior, which isn't desirable. If you criticize your child and constantly put him down or punish him, he will soon believe he isn't lovable or capable. As a parent, it is your job to ensure that your child's self-esteem and confidence don't take a back seat.

Principle #3: Offer A Choice

Everyone likes to be in control of their lives, decide and choose what they want. Well, toddlers are no different. They might not be fully-grown yet, but they understand what choice means and like choosing. A common mistake a lot of parents make is they give their children choices when interested in abiding by their decisions. With positive discipline, you're taught to offer your child the choice only when you are 100% willing to abide by his decision. The simplest way to do this is by giving the child choices acceptable to you. For instance, if your toddler throws a tantrum because he isn't allowed to play for longer, you can tell them something like, "If you have your dinner right now, you can play for 10 minutes later." You have given him a choice, which is acceptable to you. It also gives your toddler a sense of control.

Principle #4: Environment Matters

A child's behavior is often regulated by his environment. Instead of worrying too much about his behavior, concentrate on changing his environment. For instance, if your toddler's senses are constantly overstimulated because of a noisy environment, he will become cranky and throw tantrums. Understanding the cause of the tantrum- the environment- gives you more control of regulating his action. Now that you know he's throwing tantrums because he's overstimulated, you can reduce the stimulation from the environment.

Principle #5: You Are A Team

A simple principle lot of parents forget they need to work as a team with their children. If you work against a child, he will resist, and make the entire process seem like a struggle. Instead, once you work with your toddler as a team, it becomes easier to change his actions. Don't be a dictator but be a mentor. You and your child are a team and work together to change his behavior. For instance, if you are upset about your child's bedtime routine, instead of dictating terms, try to talk to him about it. With a little adjustment and understanding, you both can create a routine that works well for you. With positive discipline, you are taught how to do all this.

Principle #6: Setting Limits

We're taught that every function has a limit. What happens when a function has no limit? It either ceases to exist or doesn't work like it is supposed to. Likewise, even your toddler needs certain limits. Most limits set by parents are to regulate their toddler's behaviors are often designed, keeping their safety in mind. Ensure the limits you set up are something your child can understand. Once you set these limits, explain the consequences of breaking such limits, too. Let's assume one of the ground rules or the limits you set in the house for your toddler's safety is, "Don't run." To enforce this limit, explain what will happen if he doesn't listen to you. By explaining the importance of the limit, and the consequences of breaking it, it's more likely that your toddler will be more agreeable to following them.

It's not just about setting boundaries, but you need to be consistent too. If you are inconsistent, the child will get confused and not understand what he's supposed to do. For instance, if you tell him he isn't supposed to watch TV while eating, stick to this ground rule. No one is supposed to change this rule, regardless of the situation. There might be days when you are tired or exhausted and don't have the energy to get through dinnertime. However, it doesn't give you an excuse to allow your child to eat while watching TV. After a while, if you do this, he will soon believe there are no rules and no consequences of breaking any rules you set. With a little consistency, the child gets used to the limits. It's not just you who needs to follow these rules, although caregivers in your child's life should also be on board.

Principle #7: Gentle Reminders

Instead of demanding or ordering your toddler's compliance, you can use gentle reminders, questions, or even state facts to obtain his compliance. For instance, you might want your toddler to put his toys away after playtime. This might be a constant power struggle. There is a simple way to circumvent this. Instead of demanding his compliance by saying things such as, "You should put your toys away," or punishing him, "if you don't put your toys away, you cannot play," look for gentle reminders. Children resist because they don't like being told what to do. When you give them a command, their natural urge to resist increases. If you replace the command with a simple question or one-word reminder, it works better. To get your child to put his toys away after playtime, try reminding him, "Toys." Yes, all it takes is a single word. Instead of wasting your breath with long sentences and power struggles that leave you winded, try gentle reminders.

Principle #8: Be A Good Role Model

You are your child's first role model. Most of the behaviors that children pick up are often the culmination of all behaviors they notice in their environment. As the primary caregiver in your child's life, it's important to portray good behavior. For instance, if your child screams or shouts whenever he doesn't get something he wants, as a parent, fix this behavior. If you shout whenever you don't get something you want, you are merely contradicting what you told your child. It also causes a lot of unnecessary confusion for the kids. If you don't want your child to scream and shout, you need to model the same behavior. If he sees you doing something you told him not to, he will soon believe he need not listen to you.

Once you follow these principles and incorporate them into your parenting tactics, it becomes easier to guide your child and mold his behavior. Instead of punishing him whenever he misbehaves, positive discipline helps teach him why such behavior is undesirable. It helps shift the focus from punishments to changing his behavior for the better.

A Simple Exercise in Positive Discipline

What is misbehavior? It is the term used to describe rude, bad, or improper behavior. Only when your child consciously behaves inappropriately will such behavior be termed as misbehavior. Before you act upon it or fix it, here are simple questions you should ask yourself.

Question 1: Did my child misbehave? Did he do something wrong?

Do you think there is a problem, or maybe you are running low on energy and patience? Often, parents get upset with their children's behavior, especially when stressed, overwhelmed, or are running low on energy. For instance, there might have been instances in your past when you were upset with your toddler because he didn't put his toys away after playtime like he is supposed to. Your reaction in the situation would be different if you are overwhelmed and stressed compared to your regular reactions. If you think there is no problem, it's time to look within yourself and understand the reason for the stress and deal with it. If you strongly believe there is a problem, it brings us to the next question.

Question 2: Can my child live up to my expectations?

If there seems to be a problem, think about it for a couple of minutes. We all have certain expectations. Most problems we face in life are due to such expectations. Likewise, all parents have certain expectations. Before you get upset with your child's behavior, ask yourself:

Am I realistic about my expectations? Can my child live up to my expectations? If your expectations aren't realistic, it is time for a little reevaluation. If you believe your expectations are fair and reasonable, move on to the next question.

Question 3: Was your child aware that he was doing something wrong?

Go back and reconsider the definition of misbehavior. Actions cannot be termed as misbehavior if they are not done consciously. Therefore, try to determine if your child knew whether he was misbehaving or not. If he was unaware that he did something wrong, there is no reason to get upset with him. Instead, try to understand the following.

- What happened
- What wasn't supposed to happen
- What you expect of him and the reasons
- How it can be avoided in the future
- To prevent such behaviors in the future, offer your help and assistance

If he knew he was doing something that he wasn't supposed to and still went ahead with intentionally, it means your child misbehaved. If your child accidentally wets his bed while sleeping, it isn't an intentional act or misbehavior. If it was an accident, ask him why he did it.

Children are smarter than parents give them credit for. If you get down to his level and talk to him, he will tell you what's happening in his way. Learn to be patient with your little one, guide him, and don't punish.

Chapter Three: Positive Parenting Starts At Home (And With YOU)

Visualize this scenario: A 3-year-old toddler is throwing a tantrum because mommy cut her sandwiches as triangles instead of rectangles. She thrashes and throws up her hands and screams and cries. It seems like this tantrum will not end soon. Out of sheer frustration, the mom shouts, "Stop screaming right NOW."

Does the scenario seem familiar to you? No matter how much you love your little one and the patience you have, sometimes, calming down your toddler seems impossible. Well, all parents have been there. It's something we are all guilty of doing so don't be too hard on yourself. In the previous chapters, you introduced to the concept of positive discipline, and in this chapter, you will learn about simple ways to get started with that.

Tips to Get Started with Positive Parenting

Understand the Reasons

Why do toddlers misbehave? This is an important question all parents must ask themselves. There's always a reason for their misbehavior, even if it seems silly to you. Adults might believe the reasons to be silly, but it probably feels reasonable to the child, and that's why they behave the way they do. The simplest way to ensure any misbehavior is fixed is by finding the reason. By addressing the cause directly, you can better understand your child's needs while making him feel acknowledged and understood. Even if it doesn't solve the problem immediately, it gives your child a reason to move on without resorting to any misbehavior. Once you understand the reason, it also gives you better control over the scenario and takes the required steps to prevent the repetition of such behavior.

For instance, a toddler cries when his sibling hits him. The older sibling hit him because the little one took away his toys without asking. This is a teaching moment for both the kids. You can teach the younger one to always ask for permission before taking others' things. Similarly, you can teach the older child to regulate his emotions and talk about his feelings without physically lashing out. By teaching them the right behavior, you can reduce the chances of such instances.

Learn to be Kind and Firm

Kids often learn by mimicking the behavior of those around them, especially their primary caregivers. If a parent shouts, yells, calls the child names, or spanks him, the child soon learns it's okay to do these things when he is upset. The opposite of this is true too. As a parent, once you start showcasing kind and respectful behavior towards others, even when you are upset, it teaches your toddler to deal with a difficult situation, while being kind and respectful. When you are calm, even in difficult circumstances, it helps calm the child and increases his ability to understand what you are telling him.

Remember, there is a difference between being kind and giving in to your child's demands. A common misunderstanding is parents believe that positive discipline is like permissive parenting. Permissive parenting means giving into a child's demands whether they are reasonable or not. Don't be mean to get your point across. Learning to be kind and firm is a great way to communicate with your toddler while teaching him good behaviors. Saying no firmly and calmly is better than shouting the same at your child. Whenever you set any limits about specific behaviors such as no hitting, biting, or shouting, ensure you enforce the consequences if the rule is broken. It teaches the child about the natural relationship between actions or behaviors and their consequences. It enables the toddler to understand how to make decisions in the future.

For instance, a family rule you can establish is "No shouting or screaming." The next time your toddler shouts or screams because he didn't get something or he wants something, ignore him until he calms down. It effectively teaches him that unless he asks for something calmly and respectfully, he will not get it.

Parents Need a Timeout Too!

It isn't just the kids who need a timeout, but even parents need timeouts. Sometimes, you are tired, frustrated, irritated, or even annoyed by your child's behavior. In such instances, instead of reacting, it's better to take a timeout. Even if it's a break for about five minutes, it helps calm you down. Once you are calm, it becomes easier to deal with your child's unruly behavior. If you lose your temper in that moment and shout at him, it sends conflicting messages about not shouting when upset. Remember, the behavior you portray needs to be in harmony with the rules you set, and the established consequences.

Once you are calm, you can talk to your child about the problem. This is a good example of a teachable moment of "Do as I say, and as I do." Do you want your child to scream and shout when he's angry or upset, or do you want him to control his emotions and stay respectful? If it's the latter, you need to do the same. If you think you are about to lose it, calmly tell your child you need a couple of moments to compose yourself. Give him a timeframe of when you will come back and talk to him about the issue. The simplest way to avoid unnecessary power struggles is by walking away from the issue. Take a few deep breaths, calm yourself, and clear your mind.

Don't Be Punitive

One of the basic concepts of positive discipline and positive parenting is not to punish the child. Whenever you punish the child, it builds up a feeling of resentment, rebellion, revenge, and increases the risk of him retreating. Punishment condemns bad behavior, but it doesn't teach good or desirable behavior. Instead of doing all this, it's always better to look for nonpunitive options. A positive timeout or a time-in is a great way to implement the principles of positive discipline. A positive timeout is the exact opposite of a conventional timeout. This is not a form of punishment. In the previous chapter, it was mentioned that a child's poor behavior could be due to a stimulating environment. By using the principle of time in, you are essentially removing the child from the problematic environment. It gives your toddler a chance to calm down and stop the undesirable behavior finally.

To use a timeout, the first step is always to explain your expectations and the consequences of not meeting such expectations. For instance, if your toddler hits the family pet, tell him that such behavior will result in a timeout. Once you establish this rule and its likely consequence, it gives your toddler a chance to think about his behavior and decisions before making them. It also teaches him how to make good choices and develop his cognitive thinking abilities. If your child exhibits undesirable behavior, don't lose your cool, and calmly tell him what he did was on the right and let him sit in a quiet and safe place. Give him the time to think about his actions and the resultant consequence. Instead of being punitive, you are essentially kind and firm while correcting any undesirable behavior.

Another important thing about a time-in is you need to talk to your toddler after it ends. Explain why his previous action was undesirable or inappropriate and help him develop a better response if he experiences the same feelings in the future. This is easier said than done and requires a lot of practice and patience.

Clarity and Consistency

As your child's primary caregiver, it is your responsibility to be clear, consistent, and follow through on your promises. Before you enforce a rule, ensure that you have explained the rule to your little one and have also explained the consequences of not following the rules. Remember, the rules need to be quite small, and the consequences simple. Your toddler is still learning, and his brain is developing. If you are inconsistent, it merely creates a lot of confusion. For instance, parents often make empty threats to regulate their child's misbehavior. If you say, "No more toys for a week," when your toddler runs in the house, ensure it isn't an empty threat. If, after a day, you let him play with the toys, your threat has no value. (P.s. This isn't a good idea because it's a punishment and will not teach him good behavior and is merely an example of empty threats parents make).

If you don't follow through on what you say, your child will soon realize he need not listen to you. To avoid all this, you need to talk the talk and walk the walk too.

Learn, Learn, and Learn

Whenever your child misbehaves, don't get frustrated or worried. Instead, think of it as a teaching moment. Let us assume your toddler throws his brand-new toy during a temper tantrum. Instead of punishing him for this behavior, calmly take the toy away and don't replace it. This teaches him that breaking a toy doesn't make a new toy magically appear. Don't allow him to play with it, and certainly do not replace it. It teaches him the natural consequence of his action. The simplest way for a toddler to understand the difference between good and bad behavior is through experiences. This simple exercise will teach him that throwing his toys doesn't solve the problem, and it merely means he no longer gets to play with it.

This is also a good opportunity for you to teach him feeling words. He might not understand the words and their meanings yet, but through repetition, it becomes easier to teach different emotions he might be experiencing.

Always be Patient

Don't expect any drastic behavioral changes overnight. If this is one of your expectations, you are merely setting yourself up for disappointment. Learn to manage your expectations and consider your child's age. Remember, he is still a toddler and is learning. His prefrontal cortex, a part of the brain responsible for making sound judgments and understanding the true implication of consequences, is still in the developing stage. Therefore, it's quintessential you are patient with him. Repetition, consistency, and effort are important to teach your child good behavior and discourage undesirable behaviors. The great thing about implementing the principles of positive parenting is that it offers lifelong rewards.

As your child's primary caregiver, positive discipline also teaches you to learn to regulate your emotions and behaviors to more effectively communicate with your toddler.

Positive Discipline Techniques

Besides using time-ins, timeouts for parents, consistency, and patience, you can try some simple positive discipline techniques.

Provide Options

One effective way to encourage independence in a child from a young age is to provide options. Engaging in power struggles is seldom an efficient way to encourage good behavior; instead, it merely creates a lot of personal tiffs and unpleasantness. If you offer your child choices instead of barking commands or orders, you can avoid power struggles. This technique also helps empower your toddler. Are you wondering how this technique is an effective way of parenting? Well, you need to be smart about the choices you offer. Never offer your child choices you wouldn't follow. If you do this, it merely makes you seem inconsistent and unreliable. Instead, the choices should be simple and age-appropriate.

For instance, if you are getting ready to go out, instead of shouting at your child and saying, "We are getting late again, move it" you can say something like, "Do you want to put on your jacket first, or put on your shoes first??" In this situation, you are not concentrating on the action; instead, you are trying to move things along by giving your child choices. Both these choices are perfectly acceptable to you because it helps reduce the time he spends getting dressed. Since children love autonomy, this technique works brilliantly well.

Creating A YES Environment

Humans are naturally curious, and this curiosity is high in children. This curiosity helps them explore their surroundings and learn more about themselves and those around them. As a baby grows, his instinct of self-expression increases. This is the reason toddlers often test boundaries and push their parent's limits. It's their way of asserting their sense of freedom and understanding their environment. If a parent keeps saying, "No," all the time, the child will soon feel discouraged. Your toddler might think he is not supposed to do anything, because everything is forbidden. Instead, look for creative ways to create a healthy and safe "Yes" environment. For instance, if you have a toddler at home, baby-proofing the house is a great way to ensure the household environment is safe for your toddler to explore different things.

Your toddler's willingness to pay attention to the things you are saying increases if you don't keep discouraging him from things. For instance, if your toddler constantly breaks glass articles at home, the best thing to do is lock them up. This reduces the chances of any misbehavior, and you don't even have to say no.

Ignore Negative Behavior

Toddlers love attention; not just toddlers - all humans love attention! From a toddler's perspective, attention is good, regardless of the actions that create it. Children act out because they get the attention they think they deserve from their parents or caregivers. In such situations, the best thing you can do is ignore their negative behavior. If your child is throwing a tantrum, for no apparent reason, and all his needs are taken care of, ignore his negative behavior. He will soon tire of it and realize he will not get the attention he wants through displaying negative behavior. This technique should be used only for minor problems and nothing significant.

Fictional Characters Help

There are a lot of teaching moments while parenting a toddler. A great way to engage your toddler and teach him positive behavior (while discouraging negative behavior) is by using fictional characters. Third-party mediators, such as a puppet, toy, or characters from his favorite TV show, can be used effectively. Put up a small puppet show for your child showing good behaviors that should be used instead of undesirable ones. For instance, one puppet could hit the other while the other cries. In this situation, you can carefully explain that instead of hitting the puppet, had he merely asked the other what he wants, the situation could have been better handled. By using means of communication your toddler understands, it becomes easier to teach him good manners.

Single-Word Reminders

Most parents wrongly assume that stating their demands is the best way to get their toddlers to listen. Shouting or sternly saying, "Put your toys away!" "Stop running right now!" doesn't get the message across. Besides leaving you hoarse, it might serve no purpose at all. Instead, try using single word reminders. A principle of positive discipline is not just to fix any undesirable behavior but also to teach desirable ones. Try saying, "Walk," whenever you notice your toddler is running or if he has a tough time sharing his toys, you can say "Share." These simple reminders stated calmly will effectively convey your message while telling your toddler what he's supposed to do.

Always remember to choose your battles wisely in life; parenting is no exception. Instead of engaging in unnecessary power struggles, it is better to gently correct and redirect your child to learn better behavior.

Positive Reinforcement

Correct undesirable behavior, but also praise your toddler whenever he does something desirable. If your toddler picks up his toys after playtime with no reminders, praise his behavior using simple sentences like, "You did a good job!" or "Thank you for picking up your toys." If he is kind to others or shares his toys with his sibling, tell him, "You did great," or "I am so happy you shared your toys." Whenever you notice your toddler doing something you appreciate, convey this appreciation to him.

Stating positive statements while expressing positive emotions acts as an incentive. He will soon realize that certain behaviors will elicit a happy response from you. By giving him positive attention for his good behavior, you are reinforcing the behavior he displayed. Positive reinforcement also helps build your child's self-esteem and self-confidence. He will soon realize he can make good decisions with no external assistance. It might not seem like much to you, but it does help change and mold his behavior for the better. If a parent keeps shouting or snapping at their child for misbehaving, but doesn't reward good behavior, the child will feel discouraged sooner or later. Chances are he will withdraw himself into a shell, resent his parent, or even rebel unnecessarily.

Redirection

The attention span of a toddler is short. Whenever your toddler misbehaves, quickly redirect him to another activity. When you redirect him, it diverts his attention and effectively ends any bad behavior. For instance, if you notice your toddler is playing with something he's not supposed to, give him another toy to redirect his attention. If this technique doesn't work, you can shift from one room to another. Keep practicing the same tactic as your child grows. For instance, if you don't want your toddler watching television all the time, you can tell him he can play with his toys or take him outdoors for a while. Instead of telling him he's not supposed to do something, direct him towards a positive activity.

By following these simple techniques of positive discipline, you can effectively prevent misbehavior, encourage desirable behavior, and help your child cultivate good habits while increasing his self-confidence.

Chapter Four: Sleep Training for Your Toddler

Sleep training isn't an aspect a lot of parents even think about when they welcome their little one into their lives. However, once the baby is home, the constant feedings, diaper changes, and all the other usual responsibilities of life can quickly become overwhelming. This is when the reality of this new life sets in. Instead of the "I'll just wing it" approach, it is better to have a plan in mind. The simplest way to rectify this situation is by sleep- training your toddler. Once your toddler is sleep-trained, even you can get sufficient rest to keep doing your best as a parent.

In this chapter, you will learn about the two simple methods of sleep training, tips for using positive parenting during sleep training, and dealing with common bedtime struggles.

How to Sleep Train Your Toddler

Essentially, sleep training is teaching your toddler to sleep through the night. Initially, he might resist and will probably wake up after a couple of hours. However, if you keep at it, your toddler will soon learn to sleep through the night without disturbances.

Experts suggest it's usually ideal to start sleep training your baby when he is around 4-6 months old. By this age, babies usually have a sleep-wake routine, and the nighttime feedings also stop altogether or reduce drastically. Since no two babies are alike, don't be worried if your little one takes a while longer for sleep training. If you are unsure if your baby is ready for this step, consult a pediatrician.

So, what is the best option available for sleep training a toddler? The answer to this question depends on how your baby responds to each option; you should also be comfortable with the chosen strategy. Different experts have different opinions, and the best method is a widely debated topic. However, one thing everyone seems to agree on is the need for consistency. To sleep-train your baby, pick a strategy, and stick with it while leaving little room for flexibility. Based on your baby's responses to it, you can make the required changes. Let's learn about some different methods available.

Longer And Longer Method

If you leave the toddler in the crib or put him down for sleep on his bed and walk away, he probably cries. He is crying because he isn't used to being alone. Those who advocate this method suggest it's okay for a baby to cry until he learns to sleep. Never let your toddler cry for indefinite periods. In this method, you essentially put your toddler to bed while he is wide awake. However, even when he cries, you shouldn't comfort him or pick him up. Instead, you merely let him cry out and tire himself to sleep. This method was popularized by Richard Ferber, a pediatrician associated with the Centre for Pediatric Sleep Disorders. According to Ferber's method, it's believed the baby or toddler will sooner or later learn to soothe himself to sleep with no external support. Even if he cries for a while, he will soon put himself to sleep once he realizes no one is coming to comfort him.

This method might sound a little harsh, but it's been used for ages – and is effective. Once again, whether you want to use this method will depend on your comfort level. If your toddler cries incessantly without stopping, don't forget to check on him. Advocates suggest it will not be a traumatic experience for the baby if you let him cry himself to sleep while regularly checking on him.

No-Tears Approach

If you are uncomfortable with the previous method or it didn't work for your baby (showing no positive change within two weeks), it's time to try something new. Unlike the previous method, this approach is gradual, slowly getting your toddler accustomed to sleeping through the night without difficulty. This method is foundational upon a well-structured bedtime routine, allowing you to connect with your baby by using a comforting bedtime ritual, quickly tending to any of his requests for comfort. It will make your baby feel loved and secure while he sleeps on his own.

Start by teaching a simple-yet-consistent nap routine your toddler can follow during the day. If you regulate his naps during the day, it becomes easier to regulate his sleeping schedule at night. Try to put your toddler to sleep a little earlier than usual. Aim for anywhere between 6:30 and 7:30 PM. Many parents commonly err by allowing their toddlers to stay awake for longer, believing they will tire themselves out. Avoid this misconception! If you allow your toddler to stay past his ideal bedtime, it will merely make him cranky and increase unpleasant interactions. When you allow your baby to stay awake for longer, he'll become accustomed to staying awake at night and sleeping through the day. Simply put, if your baby is overtired or overstimulated, he cannot fall asleep at night.

Since this method is about making gradual changes, first establish an ideal bedtime for him. For instance, if your baby usually sleeps at 8:30-9 PM, don't drastically reduce it to 6:30 or 7:30 PM Instead, reduce it by 30 minutes. Keep doing this until you reach your desired time for his bedtime.

The next step is to create a relaxing and comforting bedtime ritual. Once the ritual is in place, ensure that you follow it consistently. For instance, include a warm bath, story time, lullaby, or even light music. After this, you can dim the lights, change his clothes, and put him down to sleep. The routine needs to be consistent, and there should be no deviations. This routine is not only for you; every primary caregiver in your toddler's life should follow this routine – no matter of where he is.

Come up with a phrase, word, or even a sound that acts as an external cue to signal your baby's bedtime. For instance, you can say "Shhh" gently or even use a phrase such as "It is bedtime," or "It is nighty-night-time" while you are trying to put your baby to sleep. Keep repeating this phase, word, or sound. After a while, an association will be formed in your toddler's mind, reminding him that he needs to sleep whenever you use your cue.

Another important aspect: the sleeping environment. Ensure your toddler is comfortable whenever you put him to bed. If the environment is too loud, bright, or noisy, it will overstimulate your toddler's senses, preventing him from effectively falling asleep. You can also use a white noise machine as a part of his bedtime ritual. It helps mask any background noises while creating a soothing environment, which is often helpful. While he is about to fall asleep, play some soothing music, sing a lullaby, or even read a small bedtime story. Making a bedtime story a part of his sleeping ritual gives you a chance to bond with him. Make the most of these moments because the bond you establish with him during childhood (especially early childhood), is unlike anything else.

While using this method, pay attention to his sleepy whimpers and real cries. It can be tempting to check on your little one whenever you hear any sounds from his room. Unless it's a genuine cry, don't do this. If you keep disturbing him while he's trying to sleep, he won't learn to fall asleep. However, you can check on him after an hour or two during the initial phases. Use this method to increase the time between the nighttime check-ins gradually.

Positive Parenting and Sleep Training

Here is a scenario a lot of parents might be familiar with. It is about 8 PM, and it is two-year-old Adam's bedtime. The mother says, "Adam, it is time to go to bed immediately." However, Adam seems to have other plans. He shrieks "No," and heads for the playroom. The mother follows him and says, "Adam, honey, it is time for you to sleep. Please come." Adam is vehemently shaking his head "no" and continues to play with his toys. This is the last straw, and the mother loses her cool. She picks up Adam, and he wiggles, squeals and shrieks while flailing his arms. She says, "Stop it immediately, or else!" This sends Adam into overdrive as he redoubles his efforts to get away from his mom. He cries even louder, and the emotional and physical struggle for power continues. The mother somehow gets him to brush his teeth, change his pajamas, kiss him, and puts him to bed.

Phew, she breathes a sigh of relief, thinking tonight's battle is over. Before she takes ten steps, she hears her toddler say, "Mommy, I need water." Resigned, the mother gives him the drink of water. By now, she is frustrated and tired. After this, she stiffly says, "Go to sleep now. I don't want to hear another word from you. Good night!" This leaves the two-year-old Adam crying into his pillow while he struggles to sleep.

Does this scenario sound familiar? A lot of parents might find it hard to believe, but they aren't alone; these power struggles are common. Instead of making bedtime seem like a harsh punishment or an unpleasant routine, you can quickly fix this situation by using positive discipline. While using the previous sleep training methods, here are simple things you can remember to reduce any troubles you face in this process.

If you engage in such unpleasant power struggles, it will soon take a toll on the bond you share with your toddler. It will leave you feeling guilty and frustrated while the toddler feels misunderstood. So, the simple idea is to look at the situation from his perspective.

If you look at this situation from the toddler's perspective, it gives you a better understanding of why he behaved the way he did. He was playing with his toys and having a good time. Then, an adult comes in and tells him to stop and go to sleep. Even when he said no, the adult does not listen to him. Instead, he was merely picked up and made to go through the bedtime ritual. He wasn't ready yet and was forced into doing all this. Imagine if someone did all this to you. We all expect our wishes to be respected; the toddler is no different. Instead of engaging in power struggles, it's better to understand how he might be feeling. You would feel violated, angry, frustrated, and even controlled if the roles were reversed. Many parents fail to understand that even though their toddler is not an adult, he can feel all this, like any other human.

He is an individual, wanting to be respected and understood. If you take this power away from him, it becomes difficult for him to express himself. He puts up a fight because he isn't tired or sleepy, and he doesn't enjoy feeling controlled. We don't like being ordered around either! Remember this when dealing with your toddler. Instead of commanding your toddler to do something that merely escalates the situation, there is more you can do.

Make it Special

A bedtime ritual can be a special time for bonding and strengthening the closeness and connectedness between parents and toddlers. Usually, parents are tired during the day, and at night, they are eager to tuck their little ones to sleep. For a parent, completing this task gives them a break from daily rituals and offers quiet time. However, it conveys the wrong message to the toddler. The toddler might believe his parents are trying to get rid of him by putting him to sleep. In the previous scenario, Adam's desire for a glass of water before going to bed was his way of spending more time with his mother. So, why does a child put up a fight before sleeping? It's his declaration of independence, he wants to feel closer to his parent, wants to have a sense of control over whatever happens in his life, and wants to be heard and respected.

To ensure your child goes to sleep without struggles and all his needs and wants are satisfied, *respect your needs.* You are a human and not a tireless machine. Unless you take care of yourself during the day, you cannot deal with your child's bedtime ritual without feeling frazzled. Ensure that your child's bedtime leaves you at least an hour of downtime. Once you put your toddler to bed, you need time to relax and unwind. Ideally, always start the bedtime ritual about 45 minutes to an hour before his actual bedtime. For instance, if your toddler's bedtime is 8:30 PM, start this ritual at about 7:45 PM. Also, whenever possible, both the parents should try and participate in this process. It helps bond, while eliminating unnecessary power struggles.

Routine is quintessential for a baby between the ages of 12-24 months. This provides a sense of safety and security. It's always ideal to offer your child two choices instead of commanding him to do something. It gives him control over what happens to him. For instance, you can respect his sense of time by telling him he has another 10-20 minutes of playtime left before time for sleeping. Once it's time to start the bedtime ritual, you can ask him, "Do you want to sleep with a stuffed toy or a pillow?" "Do you want to change into your batman or dinosaur pajamas?" or "Do want me, or daddy, to help you with bath time?" "Do you want to listen to a lullaby or read a story together?" "How many kisses do you want before sleeping?" In all these instances, you are essentially offering a choice where either outcome is desirable for you.

After this, you can talk to him for a few minutes about his day; what he liked most and what he didn't enjoy. Take his advice into consideration as you structure his routine. Once you have gone through all these steps, it's time to end the bedtime ritual. Remember, you shouldn't talk to him after the ritual ends. Simply leave his room after saying a pleasant good night. If your child wakes up as soon as you leave the room and returns to you, gently guide him to his bed again. Don't be harsh or stern. Instead, lovingly tell him it's time for him to sleep. You can expect such behavior during the initial days of sleep training. However, after a while, he will get used to it.

How to Deal with Nightmares and Night Terrors

The terms "nightmare" and "night terrors" might sound the same, but they aren't. Learning to deal with your toddler's nightmares and night terrors is important to tackle the problem properly. Usually, kids as young as two years can have nightmares and night terrors. These two things are commonly used by the brain to process information and emotions. They go away as the child grows.

Any unpleasant or bad, yet realistic dreams are known as toddler nightmares and disturb your little one's sleep. Your toddler might remember and recollect his nightmare once awake. He might want to discuss it with you too. Naturally, he will have a tough time falling asleep after having a nightmare. Nightmares commonly occur during the lighter stage of REM (rapid eye movement) sleep, during the early hours of each day.

Night terrors are different in subtle ways. Don't be surprised if your child seems wide-awake with his eyes open and is screaming, sleepwalking, thrashing around, panting, or sweating heavily, *while asleep*. Your toddler might scream your name, but he might not sense or feel your presence fully. You might fully remember such incidents, but your child will not. Night terrors usually occur during the deep stages of non-REM sleep. They can last for up to 45 minutes, and your toddler may fall asleep right after it.

The first step towards learning how to deal with your toddler's nightmares and night terrors is to understand the difference between them. Your toddler might even seem a little restless during the dream state, but once he is awake, he will cry, panic, or scream. He will want to be comforted by you and express himself verbally and use his words to explain what he experienced.

If your toddler is having night terrors, even when he seems wide-awake, he's fast asleep. Even if you comfort him, he cannot sense your comforting presence during a night terror. Also, he would have no recollection of such episodes.

Different reasons could cause nightmares and night terrors in kids. A common factor is children have a tough time understanding to differentiate between reality and make-believe. Any stress or anxiety they experience during their waking hours can trigger nightmares or night terrors. For instance, maybe your toddler saw a scary looking bug, is overwhelmed due to the recent move to a new city, there is a change in your work schedule, or any other major life changes. Once you deal with the underlying fear and anxiety, nightmares and night terrors will both go away.

Any erratic changes in your toddler's sleeping patterns, illness, the lack of sleep – or even certain medications – can trigger them. It's commonly believed that frequent episodes of night terrors are often associated with a family history of the same. Remember, your toddler is processing a lot of information and trying to come to terms with the reality of life. Since there is a lot to process, his senses can be overstimulated, and all this information follows him into the dream world. The duration of a toddler's sleep cycle increases with age. This also opens a window for longer dreams and, perhaps, nightmares.

If your toddler seems to be having a nightmare, the best thing you can do is comfort him with gentle, soothing, and loving phrases; even making soothing sounds will make him feel safe and secure. You can help him settle back down for sleep after a nightmare by reassuring him that everything is all right. Saying, "It was just a dream, go back to sleep, honey," might not explain enough to a two-year-old who seems startled. Instead, you can help, "Honey, you were just playing pretend in your sleep." You could also make a show of checking dark spaces in his room, such as under the bed or in the closet.

Don't minimize your child's fears. It might not be scary to you, but it is surely scary to him! Also, you might be tempted to take him back to your room and sleep in the bed with you. Avoid doing this. Instead, spend some more time calming him to sleep. There are simple ways to reduce the chance of a nightmare, such as ensuring your toddler has a soothing bedtime ritual, leaving a nightlight on, or leaving the bedroom door slightly ajar. Don't read any scary stories or allow your little one to watch scary movies right before bedtime.

Night terrors are not usually a permanent condition and go away within a few weeks. You cannot do much to stop night terrors or comfort your little one during the night terror. Attempting to wake up your little one from his night terror would leave him feeling disoriented, agitated, and confused. Likewise, don't try to hold him – even if he seems wide-awake. If he is awake, he will contact you.

Instead, if he cries, shouts, and thrashes around, it's better to let the night terror run its course. Since he cannot recollect or even remember what happened, it's likely he will go back to sleep once the night terror has run its course. Don't mention anything about the night terror the following day.

The best thing you can do to deal with a night terror is to ensure there is no stress or underlying anxiety in your child's life. Spend more time with your little one, aim for quality time together as a family, and indulge in activities he enjoys, such as reading books together, cuddling, or even bathing. Try to get his sleep schedule back on track and avoid daytime naps.

Before you seek medical help, it would be ideal for maintaining a diary to track the frequency of his nightmares and night terrors. Keep track of the time when he goes to bed, the sleep he gets every night, if he requires any object for falling asleep, the number of times he wakes up, and the duration of each break from his sleep, the number of naps during the day, and any potential triggers for nightmares. If you have tried everything to deal with his stress and anxiety, it's time to seek medical help. A pediatrician could use the information in your sleep diary to detect the problem. There isn't much you can do to stop either a nightmare or a night terror, but you can be a comforting presence in your toddler's life.

How to Deal with Bedwetting

According to "Bedwetting In US Children: Epidemiology And Related Behavior Problems" (1996), about 30% of children under the age of five years by their beds in the US alone. Most children are potty trained between two to four years, but they might not be able to stay dry at day or night until they are older. Bedwetting isn't a problematic medical condition, but it can be challenging for parents and children. Before you learn to deal with bedwetting, it's important to understand what causes it. Here are some of the probable causes of bedwetting:

- The child might be an extremely sound sleeper and doesn't wake up, even when his bladder is full.

- He probably hasn't learned how to control his bladder movements, and the connection between his brain and bladder is developing.
- The child drinks a lot of water before going to sleep, and therefore, his body produces more urine at night.
- There might be a history of bedwetting in the family. Usually, it's believed that if a child is prone to bedwetting, it's probably because one or both his parents have the same problem as a child.
- The child is ill, tired, or isn't coping well with any stress or changes at home.
- The child's bladder is small and cannot hold all the urine produced overnight.
- The final cause may be an underlying medical condition.

While you are potty training your toddler, he might have a few accidents, which isn't uncommon. He might even go for days, weeks, and months before he has an accident. If this happens, it's nothing to worry about, and you merely need to stay patient. You'll learn more about potty training your toddler in the next chapter. For now, let's concentrate on bedwetting problems. If your child has an accident after weeks of potty training, start again.

Here are questions you should consider if you're concerned about your toddler's bedwetting or your toddler has complained about it.

- Is bedwetting a family problem?
- How frequently and when does your toddler pee during the day?
- Have there been any major changes or stress at home, such as shifting to a new city, welcoming a new baby, or even marital problems?
- Does your toddler consume a lot of fluids before bedtime?
- Is there anything unusual about your toddler's urine?
- If you have successfully potty trained your toddler for six months or more and starts bedwetting, it might be due to an

underlying medical condition. Some medical troubles can trigger bedwetting suddenly are listed below:

- Changes in the frequency and timing of when your toddler urinates during the day
- If there's any disturbance with his gait, it could be a symptom of an underlying neurological condition.
- There is continuous dampness.
- The toddler is prone to bedwetting during the day and night.
- Complains about a painful burning sensation while peeing.
- Constant dribbling of a narrow stream of urine even after peeing.
- Pink or cloudy urine coupled with faint bloodstains on his underpants.

If you notice any of these signs, you need to seek medical attention immediately. These signs are often associated with any kidney or bladder trouble.

How to Manage Bedwetting?

There are simple and practical tips you can use to deal with your toddler's bedwetting successfully.

Regardless of what happens, or how tired you are, do not blame him. If you shout, yell, or belittle, it will scare and scar him. He will soon believe bedwetting is a bad thing, and he will be punished. All these things will further worsen the problem.

Learn to be sensitive to his feelings. If you make a big issue of his bedwetting accidents, he will feel embarrassed. This merely increases the embarrassment he feels after the accident. Therefore, don't make a big deal out of it and deal with it as calmly and positively. Remind him it is okay and that it isn't a bad thing.

Talk to him and be honest while addressing the situation. When you explain it isn't his fault and how most children have accidents growing up, he will feel better.

If you create a positive environment, it becomes easier to deal with the issue. One simple way to do this is by teaching him responsibility. If he wets the bed, encourage him to help you while you clean. He need not change the sheets, but he could merely move the pillows or a stuffed toy. By giving him some responsibility, he will feel more in control of the situation.

Another way to deal with it is by protecting the bed with a plastic cover over the mattress. to protect it. Do this if you are aware that your child has had bedwetting instances.

It's not just about you creating a positive environment, but everyone in the household should abide by this rule. No one should make fun of the toddler, and there should be no teasing. He probably feels embarrassed about it, and if others tease or make fun of him, he will feel worse. Such behavior from adults can worsen their bedwetting problems.

To reduce any instances of bedwetting, avoid giving your toddler a big drink before going to bed. Also, ensure he empties his bladder before sleeping. While dealing with it, you can wake him up once or twice at night and encourage him to pee. Prevention is better than cure.

How to Stop Co-Sleeping

Many parents decide to co-sleep with their infants because it's the best way to get sufficient sleep during the first couple of months. However, this isn't ideal. Whether it's for your convenience, or to promote attachment, co-sleeping is not good, especially if you want your toddler to become independent and self-reliant. If your toddler is used to co-sleeping with you for years, getting used to sleeping on his own isn't easy. The sooner you start, the easier it becomes.

To stop co-sleeping with your newborn to 18-month-old, get him used to sleep in the crib or bassinet. Whenever he needs to sleep, put him down for a nap in this space, and *nowhere else*. It might be tempting to snuggle with your little one in bed, especially when he keeps waking up for feeding or peeing. Make it a point to not cuddle with your little one on the bed until you successfully stopped co-sleeping.

Slowly transition your baby, and ensure he has a safe place to sleep. The room shouldn't be too dark, place his blankets, pillows, and stuffed toys in his sleep space. You can also use a white noise machine to ensure there are no background noises, which will keep him up. Whether you are Ferberizing or using the no-tears approach, you must teach your baby to fall asleep independently. Use the tips discussed in the previous sections to create a soothing bedtime ritual while you transitioned from co-sleeping to sleeping in his crib or bassinet.

How can you stop co-sleeping with your baby between the ages of 18-48-months? If your toddler has been sleeping with you for 18 months, he is likely used to it. Now, you cannot just decide one fine day it needs to stop, and simply put him to sleep in his room. It doesn't work, and it will be a drastic change for your little one. The shock of it would prevent him from sleeping comfortably at night. Instead, start slowly. Talk to your little one about how he needs to sleep in his room. You could call it the "big kids" room and explain that he needs a room to himself *since he is a big kid.*

You can make the change easy by putting a positive spin on it. Don't forget to go through the soothing and consistent bedtime ritual every night. Ensure you set some time aside for cuddling and bonding with your little one. If you stick to this routine and encourage him to sleep in his room, he will soon get its hang. Don't forget to use the sleeping techniques and tips discussed in the previous sections. Another simple way to ensure that your child feels comfortable at night is by reassuring him that everything is okay and leaving the room. Even if he cries for a while, he will soon stop.

Sleep training takes time, effort, and patience. If one method doesn't work, try another approach.

Chapter Five: Potty Training Your Toddler

A major developmental milestone in your toddler's life is the end of using diapers and wipes. It might make your heart leap with infinite joy because your toddler has finally learned to stop "doing his business" in his diapers. Now, the next logical step you need to concentrate on is potty training him. This requires the consistent effort of all caregivers in your toddler's life. In this chapter, you will learn about identifying the signs your little one is ready to start potty training, positive parenting tips to make potty training more manageable, and how to overcome the common potty training problems you might face.

How to Start Potty Training

Signs of Readiness
Ideally, toddlers between the age of 18 and 24 months are often ready to be potty trained. However, there is no rush, and since every child grows at his own pace, don't worry even if he is three years old. If he takes a while longer to start, it is okay. No matter what age you start, here are signs of readiness you should watch out for.

One of the first signs of potty readiness is a dry diaper for over two hours. It essentially shows your little one's ability to hold it for a few hours. This is a positive sign, and don't forget to keep checking his diapers every two hours when he is between 18-24 months.

Another common sign is that your toddler seems interested in using the toilet: if he *likes* to sit on the potty, talks about using the potty, or is eager to use it, get started immediately. Toddlers are curious, and his readiness could be showcased by his curiosity of using the potty like grownups.

Around this stage, your toddler might also express a desire to go to the bathroom and can follow simple instructions you give him. If he can pull down or up the elastic of his underpants before or after going with no help, that's a readiness signal. If you notice he is reluctant to be potty trained, even after showing these signs, it isn't anything to worry about. It is okay to wait for a while longer and allow your child to be fully prepared for this step.

Other signs of readiness include regular bowel movements, any vocal expression about his wanting to go to the bathroom. If your toddler keeps happily broadcasting that time for him to pee or poop, encourage him to go to the toilet. Another sign: he no longer wants to stay in damp or dirty diapers.

Start Talking

If you are happy, cheerful, and enthusiastic about potty training, all these positive emotions will rub off on your little one. Therefore, always maintain a positive attitude while talking about potty training; be encouraging. Start the conversation about potty training by encouraging your little one to sit on the toilet, even when clothed. It helps build familiarity. You can also place some of his toys in the bathroom to make it seem less intimidating. It might not seem like much to an adult, but it is a major change for your little one. Therefore, try to view the situation from his perspective. Before you encourage him to sit on the potty, you can show how it's done by being fully clothed.

Another way to put a positive spin on this new change is by offering him choices, allowing him to feel more in control. It also reduces any struggles you might encounter . However, be mindful of the options you are offering. If you ask him a question like, "Do you want to use the toilet?" be prepared to receive "no," as an answer. Instead, you can ask him, "Do you want to wear your big kid underpants?" Or "Do you want to try on your new underpants?" It's likely he will be tempted to do these things.

If your little one looks scared, anxious, or resists no matter how much you try, take a break. You can attempt the training later. Unless he is ready, potty training will become an uphill battle.

He might also take an interest in seeing other kids his age using the bathroom – or even other adults. Use this technique only if you are 100% comfortable with it. For instance, you can casually lower your trousers and sit on the toilet and talk excitedly and animatedly about the process. Explaining the process and what you are feeling reduces any fear and uncertainty your little one might be feeling. If you love reading stories to your little one, you can both bond with him and encourage him with stories concerning potty training. It helps expose your child to characters experiencing the joys of this new step while entertaining at the same time.

Parents Need Help Too

Remember, it's not just your child who needs to be ready, even you should be consistent. You are your child's guide, and you need to be with him every step of the way. During the initial days, parents are excited and enthusiastic about the process and eagerly tend to their child and make sure he uses the bathroom regularly. However, when you get busy, you might tend to slide on this habit. Understand that every child develops at his own pace; some might get the hang of it right away, while others need more help.

If any other major changes happen in your toddler's life, wait for a while before potty training. Toddlers take a while longer to get used to change than adults do and process it differently. Some examples of big changes include welcoming a baby home, sleep training him, or moving to a new house.

During the initial stages, it is ideal to set a potty timer to remember it is time for your toddler to go. Ideally, set the timer for anywhere between 30 minutes-two hours, according to your child's needs. You can also use this technique to casually remind your child he is wearing "big kid underpants" and not his usual diapers. You could say something like, "You are wearing your big kid underpants and should use the toilet whenever you need to go." Ensure that your tone stays upbeat and excited while you talk about things related to potty training. Don't forget to get your toddler involved in this entire process. For instance, if you are using a timer to remind yourself, encourage your toddler to understand what it means when the timer goes off. Once it goes off, you could ask him, "What time is it?" The first couple of times, you need to answer the question yourself with an excited "It's potty time." After a couple of tries, your toddler will get the hang of it. Even if you don't hear the timer go off, he will remind you once it does.

It's not just using the toilet; you also need to teach him good personal hygiene. After he is done, don't forget to encourage him to wash his hands. This is one habit that will stay with him throughout his life.

Tips to Prepare Your Toddler for Potty Training

Your toddler might be ready to start potty training, but don't throw his diapers away, at least, not yet. Transitioning from diapers to using the toilet isn't simple! Consider the following tips.

Before you get started with potty training, motivate your child by stating the different benefits of using the toilet like an adult. For instance, you could say something like, "You are going to wear big-boy underwear" "New underwear is fun" or "You can start flushing just like mommy and daddy do!" However, be careful when using positive phrases for potty training. For instance, you should never mock your toddler's previous habits or make them seem babyish. If you do this, it will demotivate him and even make him resist the process.

Your toddler is growing, and if you acknowledge and appreciate his growth, it helps encourage positive behavior. Whenever you notice grownup behavior, such as drinking from his cup without spilling, willingly sharing his toys, or eating on his own, compliment or appreciate it. Don't expect any sophistication at this age. His behavior might not be as polished as an adult's behavior, but he is getting there. When he knows that you support his growth and development, his willingness to portray such behavior also increases. However, if you put too much pressure on him to start acting like a grownup, is it will prove regressive, and he may begin to miss the simple ways of his baby days.

You could also show him how to use the potty. Most behaviors and actions a toddler learns are mimicking those around him. You can explain a lot about squatting, doing his business, wiping, flushing, and washing hands, but it might not be as effective as show and tell. Instead of lecturing about all these things, show him what he needs to do. You could bring him with you to the bathroom and demonstrate. If you are uncomfortable doing this in front of him, you could demonstrate these actions while fully clothed. You can also use his favorite stuffed toy to explain the process.

Dress your toddler for potty training success, the pull-down and pull-up movements. If there are too many buttons or tricky hooks to remove, it complicates the process. Instead, choose stretchy clothes that can be easily pulled up and down. Encourage him to practice these maneuvers before potty training. Ask him to pull his pants down and pull them up. You can also make a game out of it by timing how long he takes to repeat these maneuvers. This makes it easier for him to repeat these maneuvers when it's time to go.

You need to slowly, but surely, bridge the gap between diapers and transitioning to using a toilet like an adult. The room where his potty is placed can be used to change his diapers. If you introduce the change in stages, it becomes easier to transition from using diapers to the toilet. After he soils his diaper, bring him to the washroom to see you flush the contents away. Don't be surprised if the flushing sound startles your little one. If he gets startled, simply dump it for now, and you could teach him about flushing later.

You also need a training potty. The design you choose should be strong, sturdy, and durable. If it is a flimsy structure, it might tip over when your child gets on it. To make things more exciting and increase your child's motivation to use the potty, you can go shopping for it. The more involved your child is in this process, the easier it is to potty train him. If he refuses to use the baby potty and wishes to use the adult toilet, you can purchase our potty seat, which could be attached to the toilet. If required, you might also need a small stool or footrest he can use to boost himself onto the toilet.

Tips to Get Started With Potty Training

Once you follow the different tips and suggestions in the previous section, it's time to get started. The previous steps helped lay down the groundwork required to successfully potty train your little one.

Instead of diapers, it's time to switch to pull-ups. During the initial stages, it would be ideal to choose disposable ones. The main advantage of using pull-ups is that he can easily pull them down like actual underpants - a helpful training tool. Also, even if he has an accident, the absorbent pull-up varieties will readily absorb his pee or poop and be easily removed. Once he gets the hang of using the toilet whenever he needs to go, you can shift to regular washable training pants.

During this stage, observe your little one closely. His body signals become apparent whenever he needs to go. If you pay attention to his cues, it becomes easier to train him and reduce any accidents. Some telltale signs of using the loo include straining or fidgeting. If you suspect he needs to use the toilet, you could ask him. If you were a little late in identifying the cues and already done the job, place him on the potty after lowering his underpants to establish the connection between the toilet and the urge to go.

You can also encourage your toddler to check for dryness as you used to when he was younger. It not only gives him a sense of control but also encourages self-confidence and self-esteem. It is a small task, but acknowledge and appreciate his effort. For instance, if he tells you he is dry, hug him, or pat him on the back. Let him know that he did something good, and you appreciate it. Positive reinforcement during potty training plays an enormous role. Likewise, don't lose your calm and patience if he has an accident.

To teach your toddler to learn of his body's signals, encourage him to bare his bottom. You can also let him walk around with a bare bottom in the yard or a room with washable floors. It becomes hard to ignore the pee or poop if there are no diapers or underpants to mask them. Also, ensure that his training potty is nearby if he needs to use it.

Ensure that you keep your toddler motivated during this stage. Keep gently reminding him it is a sign he is growing up. Whenever he uses the potty, tell him this is what all the big kids and adults too. Now that he is a big kid, he also needs to use the potty. During the initial stages, offering a small and tangible reward goes a long way. For instance, you could put a smiley sticker on his calendar whenever he uses the toilet. Or maybe put a penny in his piggybank when he does the deed. However, you need to slowly phase out the tangible rewards to prevent your little one from becoming dependent. You can replace it with praise and appreciation. After a while, this helps develop his inner motivation to use the toilet like grownups.

You need to remind him when he needs to go, but don't keep nagging him. If you constantly nag him, he probably will resist or stops telling you when he needs to go. Likewise, never force your toddler to keep sitting on the potty forcefully or for longer than required. If you force him to sit on the potty when he doesn't want to, even when you know he wants to go, it creates negative feelings toward using the toilet. Once this negative association takes root in his mind, undoing, it becomes challenging.

Even if your toddler is enthusiastic about potty training, it can take a while before he gets the hang of it. Becoming proficient at it is not an overnight process and can take several weeks. Sometimes, it feels like you're taking one step forward and two steps back. This is common, and the only thing you need to remember is not to lose your patience. If you are loving, patient, and positive about the entire process, the journey becomes easier for you and your toddler. Also, don't set unrealistic expectations about the time required. Unrealistic expectations not only increase the stress on your toddler but also burden the relationship. Never punish, shame, or overreact if he has an accident. Do not these things if he doesn't want to use the toilet yet.

Never deny your toddler any drinks because you want to potty train him. You can reduce the number of fluids he consumes before bedtime, but not at other times. Even if he has an accident, remember to spin it positively. As to fluids, it's unfair and unhealthy to deny these; instead, steadily increase his intake of fluids, creating more teachable moments.

Positive Parenting and Potty Training

Don't Forget Your Manners

"Please," "thank you," and "sorry." Never forget these three golden words. All it takes is a little courtesy to get your toddler's attention. If you want him to use potty, use "please" in the sentence, so it doesn't seem like a command. However, do not say something that would prompt your toddler to say "no." For instance, you could tell him, "Please sit on the potty, and once you're done, we can go out and play." A sentence like this is not only courteous, but it also offers an incentive, which could act as an encouragement. Now, the toddler knows he needs to sit on the potty and do his job, and then it's time to play.

Don't Shame The Toddler

Never shame your toddler for his behavior. If he doesn't listen to you, change your approach, but don't belittle him. Embarrassing or reprimanding him is not effective, and it merely increases the chances of accidents. As adults, we don't like to be shamed, and the same logic applies to your toddler too. He is a little human. Do not admonish him if he has an accident or doesn't use the toilet as you asked him to; instead, offer loving and gentle guidance. Instead of reprimanding or shaming him, choose the effective approach of letting him know what you want him to do. For instance, you can get frustrated when he has an accident. Do not say things like, "Why didn't you tell me that you had an accident? Look at the mess you made." Such harsh sentences will effectively prevent him from trying in the future. Also, he might withdraw or regress. Instead, try saying something like, "The next time you need to go, let me know." In this way, you've not only offered him guidance, but have also shown him *what* you want him to do.

Using Praise

Using praise is a great way to motivate your little one for potty training. While you use praise, ensure it is specific and enthusiastic but does not place too much stress on a specific outcome. A simple form of praise could be a loving kiss or a hug, a pat on the back, or even a high-five. These gestures are encouraging and help your toddler feel confident. It also increases the chances of him repeating the same actions.

The praise you offer needs to be immediate and not given at a later stage. If he does something that makes you happy, tell him immediately. If you wait until later, he might not even remember the event.

Use praise but use it sparingly. Ensure it is used for a special occasion, and only when your toddler truly deserves it. This doesn't mean you should be stingy; it only means you need to choose the events wisely. If you keep praising him all the time, you will inadvertently turn your toddler into a praise junkie. The next time he does something, he will expect praise, and when he doesn't get what he thinks he deserves, he may feel upset and cranky.

Establish And Follow A Routine

Toddlers thrive when they have a routine. An established routine gives them a sense of security, but it also helps them understand what others expect of them. Therefore, it's important to establish a routine and stick to it consistently. Even if your child need not go, create a routine to teach him potty timings. For instance, as soon as he wakes up in the morning, gives him about five minutes, take him to the toilet, and sit him down on it. Likewise, ensure that you do the same after his mealtime, naps, and playtime. Once you have established a potty routine, ensure that everyone in the household follows it too.

Learn To Be Patient

Patience is a virtue, and it is critical in parenting. For anything associated with your little one, you need to be patient. Your toddler is new to this world, and he is slowly learning the ways of it and bound to make a few mistakes. Learn to keep your calm and don't take your frustration out on these little souls. If you notice that you both are constantly at loggerheads and your temper is flaring, step back and take a break. You can resume this activity after a week or two.

Support System

We all need a little support occasionally. You can rely on your pediatrician for support while potty training your little one. Besides this, you can talk to other parents, join online support forums, and chat rooms. When you know there are other parents experiencing this stage, you will feel infinitely better about your situation. When you talk to others, you might stumble across some advice you didn't think of before.

Countdown Calendar, And Sticker Charts

Treat stickers as rewards for whenever your child successfully uses the toilet. Place these little paper incentives on a chart in his bedroom, allowing him to place them himself whenever he uses the restroom to pee or poop.

You can also use a countdown calendar to begin the date when you want to start potty training. Ensure that you are upbeat about it and get your little one excited for potty training. For instance, if you wish to start potty training five days from now, mark the date on the calendar with a big x. Tell him it's an event you are excited for. As soon as you wake up your little one in the morning, tell him "5 days to go until you are a big boy!" the next day, it would be "4 days to go until you are a big boy," and so on. During this period, use a lot of positive talk about potty training. Tell him that big boys wear underpants and use the potty to do their business. Don't make it seem intimidating and keep things light and pleasant.

Overcome Potty Training Problems

This section will introduce you to a few other common potty training issues, and ways to overcome them.

Difference Between Pee And Poop

The toddler might understand that he needs to empty his bowels but doesn't recognize the urge to pee. Toddlers can take a while before they have complete control over their bladders. Meanwhile, there might be accidents that you need to prepare yourself for.

Squatting And Peeing

All toddlers - not just the girls - might be comfortable squatting and peeing instead of standing. If you notice your child doing this, don't worry. He might have observed his family members sitting down to pee, and he is doing the same. Once he grows older, he could learn how to stand and pee. This is up to him, and don't change this right now. The only thing you need to concentrate on is whether your toddler can *recognize his urge* to pee or empty his bowels.

A Little Too Curious

Toddlers are naturally curious, and this curiosity of theirs is healthy. Usually, it isn't anything you need to worry about. However, if your little one gets a little too curious and plays with his feces, it's time to intervene. You don't have to be stern or angry while intervening; this is common curiosity – he isn't acting out any ill ulterior motives.

Therefore, carefully handle the situation. For instance, you could tell him, "This is not a toy," or "You should not play with this."

Dealing With Accidents

Dealing with accidents is an important part of potty training. Don't get upset when he has an accident; instead, treat it lightly, taking it in stride and moving right along. If you concentrate too much on it or make a big deal out of it, you will frighten, intimidate, embarrass, and belittle your little one!

Resists Pooping

If your child is resisting, he needs more time before he is ready for potty training. Whenever you notice he is about to pee or poop, take him to the potty area. Ensure that he is seated on it for a few minutes and no longer. Explain the process to him and tell him it's natural. Your words of encouragement and loving praise will give him the motivation required to be potty trained.

Scared Of The Toilet

Toddlers can fear the toilet itself. Yes, the big shiny white bowl that makes noises is a very intimidating object for a toddler. He could be scared of being sucked into it when he flushes. The sound of flushing could startle him. Both these things are common, and they can be easily overcome. For instance, you can stand with him on the site and encourage him to flush down toilet paper pieces. Once he realizes he has complete control over this object, the fear will likely resolve.

Flushed Away Poop

Don't be too surprised if you notice that your child is upset when he sees his poop being flushed away. Little children often believe their poop to be a natural part of the body instead of the waste it produces. Therefore, parting with it might be a scary instance for them. So, spend some time with your little one and explain that he need not hold onto the poop, and it is just his body eliminating the things it doesn't need.

Asks For Diapers

If you notice that your toddler is asking for diapers when he needs to have a bowel movement, but then goes to a special place to do this, it's a sign he isn't ready for potty training. He can recognize his physical urge to defecate but isn't mentally or emotionally ready for potty training. Don't think of it as an absolute failure. The first step of potty training is to teach your child to recognize these natural urges. Now that he recognizes it, it's okay to take some more time before you start potty training. So, keep a positive attitude and praise him for understanding when he needs to go.

Wrong Time

Sometimes, your toddler pees or poops after you remove him from the toilet (this usually happens right after you he leaves it.) It can be frustrating, but please, keep your calm. It also occurs during the early stages of potty training. It is a part of the process, and it will take your little one some time to understand how to relax the muscles in his bladder and bowel. Once he gains better control over these things, these accidents will happen less frequently. If this keeps happening and makes them uncomfortable, take a break from potty training; he isn't ready for this process.

Signs Of Regression

Stress can be a regressing factor. If your child is stressed, he will likely return to the previous level of development he is comfortable with. Shifting to a new house, illness, having guests at home, or even changing from sleeping in his crib to a bed could be stressful. If you notice he wants to use his diapers but has several accidents, it's time to stop potty training for a while. Give it a break, and you can start again after a few days. If you keep going while the child is stressed, it will prompt him to withdraw further and speed up the regression.

Comfort Level

Sometimes. toddlers are comfortable using the toilet only in the presence of certain individuals. This is normal, and to be expected. If you are the only one he is comfortable within the bathroom, don't worry. You need to withdraw yourself from the room gradually, and he will soon get used to doing the deed without help. For instance, you can offer to help him undress and walk away from the bathroom.

You can reassure him by waiting outside and offer words of encouragement if required.

While potty training, prepare to deal with some bumps along the way, it will not be easy, but it is doable. By following the simple tips and suggestions discussed in this section, you can successfully potty train your toddler within a few weeks.

Chapter Six: Dealing with Tantrums and Misbehavior

Watching your little one grow is an incredible experience. From his first laugh to the first uncertain steps he takes and the words he utters, the journey is riddled with beautiful and unforgettable moments. However, certain things are not as pleasant, yet still a part of the growing up process. For instance, you might have heard about the terrible twos. Most parents dread this age. Are you wondering why? The period between 24-36 months is exciting for your toddler, and this is when they realize they are separate entities from the adults around them. Dealing with toddler tantrums is a part of a parent's job description, so be prepared.

This doesn't mean you need to accept all tantrums your toddler throws and don't correct his behavior. Dealing with tantrums and changing his behaviors for the better is an essential aspect of positive parenting. There are simple yet effective ways to deal with your toddler's tantrums without resorting to punishing him. Often, parents scream and shout at their toddlers while they are throwing tantrums. Before you do this, it's important to understand *why* he is throwing a tantrum, and what you can do to fix it? Once you have the answers to these questions, maintaining peace at home becomes easier, and it also helps your toddler deal with his emotions, reducing the chances of undesirable behavior.

Why Do Toddlers Misbehave?

A common question many parents fail to answer or even think about is *why* their toddlers misbehave.

Visualize this scenario. Your two-year-old kid starts screaming at the grocery store, saying, "Mommy, I just want candy!" You tell him to calm down and that he cannot have a candy bar. Before you even realize what's happening, he is screaming, shouting, and crying like there's no tomorrow. You look at him aghast, trying to understand what happened while everyone at the store is staring. Your tiny toddler has now become the center of attention, and you are utterly baffled. This is a common scenario that we've probably all watched play out. Don't think of it as a failure on your part as a parent, but it's time to consider why your toddler is misbehaving.

All the crying, screaming, shouting, whining, and kicking are a part of toddler's tantrums. These are perhaps the only ways the little ones can communicate with the adults around them. Remember, your child hasn't yet learned how to effectively communicate what he or she is feeling. At two or three years old, toddlers begin to assert themselves and are inclined to communicate their likes and dislikes. They also try to act as independently as they can. During this period, toddlers are also learning to communicate and develop their communication skills to express what they want or need, or their ideas. It is a period of growth, but the toddler is still too young to understand the logic and has a hard time understanding the concept of self-control and patience. So, even seemingly harmless words such as "no," or "don't" can set him off.

In this age group, toddlers are learning to handle their strong emotions. Even adults have a tough time managing their big emotions; can you imagine how overwhelming it would be for a toddler? For instance, we have the luxury of explaining what we're feeling and the reasons for the same. However, a toddler is still learning to do all these things. If he cries or throws a tantrum, it's probably because it's the only way he knows to communicate. It doesn't mean tantrums are acceptable. However, understanding the reasons he is acting out is a starting point.

Do not jump to the conclusion that your toddler is a brat because he throws tantrums. Babies have absolutely no awareness about anything at the time of birth. As they grow, they learn new things. On the other hand, a two-year-old might have learned to walk. He probably wants to explore the world, is learning and fine-tuning his motor skills, and has picked up vocabulary. Armed with all this, the toddler would look for opportunities to improve these skills and use them.

So, what seems to be the problem? While doing all this, toddlers look to their parents for support, safety, comfort, and encouragement. A toddler might be proud of his artwork. However, the parent might be upset upon discovering that the canvas for their toddler's artwork is the freshly painted wall in the living room. He might try to stand on his highchair, while the parent removes him and places him on the floor. A parent does these things trying to protect their toddler, who might feel frustrated that instead of encouragement, all his efforts are met with "No," "Stop!" "Don't do that!" and so on. As a parent, you might not realize it, but all these things trigger disappointment, anger, frustration, and a lot of internal turmoil. Essentially your toddler is dealing with a bunch of foreign emotions and isn't coping well. If your toddler throws a temper tantrum, think of it as an outlet for his strong emotions.

If your toddler has a meltdown down because you don't understand his words, says yes when he means no, gets upset, throws his toys around, doesn't like settling for substitutes, and acts out when frustrated, it means he is struggling to cope with his emotions. He is also learning to assert his independence. It essentially means he is trying to do more things on his own but gets upset or frustrated when he cannot do it or is prevented from doing it. For instance, don't be surprised if your toddler screams and shouts when you try feeding him because he is making a mess while eating. What do you think went wrong? As a parent, you are probably trying to help him eat. From a toddler's perspective, you are taking away his independence. The reasons for toddler's tantrums are often simple and obvious. All it takes is a little patience to understand it. Once you understand the reason, tackling it and preventing such meltdowns becomes easier.

Even science backs these claims. Whenever your toddler is overcome by a powerful emotion such as anger, frustration, or disappointment, his amygdala (part of the brain), the center of emotional responses, is triggered. This releases a burst of stress hormones that further intensify the toddler's emotions. The anguish it unleashes in the form of emotional discord is like physical anguish one might experience. Unless the brain's prefrontal cortex is developed - the region that regulates strong emotions – the child cannot fully control himself. This region is still in the developing stages, and therefore, toddlers throw tantrums.

Another aspect of brain biology that needs to be considered: the brain's thinking area isn't fully mature until the individual is in their mid-20s. This is another reason that not only toddlers, but even older kids have trouble regulating their emotions. Toddlers between the ages of three and five can have such tantrums, as they are just an outlet for emotions. Once you teach your little one to regulate his emotions, the tantrums will eventually resolve.

There are billions of neurons present in the brain at birth. These neurons need to be connected to facilitate rational and logical thinking. However, babies have only a few neural connections (or "synapses.") Synapses help regulate emotions and facilitate thinking, reasoning, and decision-making, and are *only developed through life experiences.* Understanding and regulating one's emotions during a temper tantrum or an outburst helps establish the much-needed synaptic connections. If your toddler learns the right way to handle his emotions without getting overwhelmed, the neural pathways developed in his young brain will stay with him as he grows.

Once he learns to manage his options and stress, it becomes easier for him to become assertive and independent later in life. If he isn't given the right opportunities or is denied a chance to regulate his emotions, it will harm his emotional and mental development. For instance, if you punish your toddler for having an outburst or throwing a tantrum, it prevents him from learning how to handle stress and other emotions. The child might internalize his feelings and suppressing certain emotions, which can later cause severe emotional and mental trouble. It's not just internalization of problematic issues; externalizing it through aggressive behavior or substance abuse later in life is undesirable. This is one reason childhood years are considered the formative years of a person's life. Therefore, it's quintessential that parents deal with their little one's outbursts and tantrums without doling out punishment.

Dealing with Toddler Tantrums

Now that you understand the reasons for a toddler's tantrums and the brain chemistry at work, let's look at simple tips to deal with them.

Don't Try To Reason

A common mistake parents make while dealing with their toddler's outburst is trying to reason with the child. You cannot reason with your toddler during a tantrum. Your toddler will neither understand, much less listen to, logical reasoning. Instead of getting frustrated in this, take a break. Don't engage with him but *do* remove him from any situation that might harm him. Allow the tantrum to run its course, and there will be plenty of time for explanations later. Your toddler is in no state of mind to listen to anything you say. So, save your breath and prevent the situation from escalating by disengaging.

Offer A Distraction

A toddler's attention span is limited; he's easily distracted. You can effectively use this to your advantage. If your toddler is upset because he cannot go out and play, offer a distraction by asking him if he would want to play with his favorite toy. Your offer should be something you can live with. Don't offer distractions as a form of emotional resolution. Instead, think of it as a means to calm your toddler.

Staying Calm And Positive

It is easy to lose your cool or get upset when your toddler throws a tantrum. If everyone in the room were shouting and screaming, would it help? No, that merely escalates the situation. To avoid this, stay calm, composed, and positive. Your toddler is sensitive to your emotions and vibes. If you get upset, it merely intensifies the emotions he feels, which triggered the tantrum. It will do you good to remember you are the adult and you must act like one. Staying calm and positive differs from giving in. You don't have to smile, but don't frown or look disappointed.

Restore And Emotional Balance

A toddler's emotional brain is like the gas pedal of a car, and the thinking brain is the brake. Living through toddlerhood is like driving with no brakes. Now, a tantrum is a runaway car. To disengage such behavior, you can offer a hug. The physical act of lovingly hugging your toddler during a tantrum is like disengaging the transmission in the runaway car without brakes. Don't wrongly believe that giving a hug is a reward for his behavior. Instead, think of it as a tool to disengage the transmission system.

The next time your toddler cries, screams, kicks, and flails his arms, try hugging him. This physical gesture prevents him from acting out or harming himself accidentally. Communicate the simple message, "You are loved, and I understand you." Never underestimate the power of hugging; it works.

Don't Use Punishment

Never punish your toddler for having a tantrum. If you punish him when he acts out, he will believe he shouldn't express his emotions and may suppress them instead. Visualize this scenario: you are in a lot of pain to the extent that you start writhing on the floor. If your loved one shouts or punishes you for expressing your pain, how would you feel? Chances are, you will feel more miserable than you did before. Also, what is the message you'll receive? You probably feel that others don't care about you and are inconsiderate of your feelings. The next time your toddler is throwing a tantrum, remind yourself of this scenario. A principle of positive parenting is to view the situations from your toddler's perspective instead of yourself. Every situation can be viewed from multiple perspectives. By changing your perspective, you get a better understanding of what your toddler must be feeling.

Therefore, don't punish him for acting out. Instead, gently correct his behavior later. If you believe a tantrum will not end soon and intervention is required, give him time in. Time-in differs from a timeout. In a time-in, you are physically shifting your toddler from the environment that triggered the tantrum to a calm and peaceful place. Sit with him during this period, and just be there. He will calm down, and once he is calm, you can talk to him again.

Teach Emotional Vocabulary

Toddlers often throw tantrums because they cannot deal with all the emotions they feel and experience. By teaching him emotional vocabulary or improving his communication skills, you can reduce tantrums. Even if you cannot immediately reduce the number of such incidents, it will teach him to manage the situation better. Don't try teach him vocabulary for better self-expression during the tantrum; instead, allow him to calm down and let the emotional tornado settle. For instance, if your toddler threw a tantrum because he was denied something, you can explain different ways he could better express himself the next time.

After he calms down, you can narrate the circumstances that led to the tantrum and how he behaved. Using simple words to explain this to your child helps develop important neural connections required for managing emotional situations. You can also try and explain how you feel whenever he throws a tantrum. For instance, you can say, "I feel sad when you throw a tantrum."

Simple feelings such as anger, sadness, happiness, excitement, and upset can be taught. You can also use imaginary characters and his favorite stuffed toys to explain all this. For instance, you could tickle him, and when you both laugh, you could say it means to be this happy. Likewise, if someone cries, it means they are sad. By teaching him these simple words, you enhance its ability to deal with his emotions while expressing his needs.

Prevent A Tantrum

Prevention is always better than cure the same stands true for tantrums too. Here's a simple acronym you can use to prevent a tantrum or reduce their occurrences. The acronym is HALT, and it stands for hunger, anger, loneliness, and tiredness. There are certain physical factors such as tiredness and hunger that can trigger a tantrum. It's not just toddlers, and even adults tend to get a little cranky when they are hungry or tired. Even if just one of the physical factors discussed in the acronym occurs, it acts as a trigger. The simplest way to avoid all these things is by establishing a proper bedtime routine for your child to get his good night's sleep. Ensure that your child is well-fed and has his meals and snacks on time. If you realize he has agitated, for no apparent reason, you could offer him a snack. Other triggers such as boredom, stress, disappointment, frustration, and anger can also effectively trigger tantrums.

As an example, if you know your child will be disappointed if you don't take him to the zoo as promised, be sure to have an alternative in mind. When that moment comes, offer an equally good distraction. Maybe you can go to the park, play his favorite game, or watch a movie together.

All the tips in this section are based on the simple concepts of positive parenting. Don't use these tips only during a tantrum; use some for preventing it in the first place! If you teach your child about emotions and communicating them, it becomes easier to understand what he needs. It also helps the child calm down when he knows he is understood.

Chapter Seven: Encouraging Creativity And Imagination

Toddlers are creative and imaginative. They might lack logical thinking and reasoning, and they make up for it with their creativity and imagination. As your toddler's primary caregiver, encourage him to develop and explore the potential of his creativity, remembering that this gift is also crucial for problem-solving. In the previous chapter, we talked about the prefrontal cortex being in the developing phase during toddlerhood. The more he exercises his mental muscles, the stronger they become. This section provides simple games and activities for your toddler to enhance his creativity and imagination.

By the time your toddler is 24-months old, his creativity and imagination will develop in full swing. It's likely very entertaining and amusing to watch him unleash these characteristics. He might plop a blob of paint on a piece of paper and call it a cat or wave a straw and pretend he's a knight! He could probably tell you he plans on visiting the moon with such conviction it puts a smile on your face.

Toddlers might not understand logic or rational thinking, but they certainly make up for all this in imagination. For learning, imagination is a powerful tool that can improve his overall skills. You can improve your child's social, verbal, and thinking skills by engaging in pretend plays. You can narrate scenarios, read stories together, or act out characters from his favorite cartoons using his toys to create "shows" together. A great thing about encouraging your toddler's creativity is that it's the first step towards teaching him problem-solving skills. Unless he can think outside the box, dealing with obstacles in life can become a little overwhelming.

Exploring his imagination and creativity also gives him a chance to understand what the grown-up world is like. His artistic inclinations can fine-tune his motor skills while playtime can teach him the importance of teams. All these things give him the tools to express his emotions and feelings. Unless given an opportunity, a child cannot explore his potential. This is where parents need to step in and help their little one explore!

During toddlerhood, a primary goal is encouraging your child's creativity and imagination. It doesn't matter whether he wishes to pursue these talents later; this helps prepare his mind to answer questions, solve problems, and makes him more mentally agile. The mind is also a muscle, and the body exercises, the stronger it becomes. You need no expensive supplies or toys to teach all these things. All it takes is genuine interest and praise to increase his creativity. Even simple props such as crayons, colorful markers, papers, and water will come in handy. It's not just your child who will enjoy this – you can too. Whenever you engage in playtime together, it gives you a chance to bond with him. This bond will stay with him forever, and it is something he will come to enjoy and look forward to. You are helping your child grow and learn and equipping him with important life skills.

Here are simple ways to encourage your child to explore his creative side and allow his imagination to run wild.

Spend more time playing with your little one. Whenever you play, ensure you always follow his lead and let him believe he is the leader. Whether he is the knight in shiny armor fighting off the evil dragon or flying to the moon in his cardboard "rocket," he simply follows what he's doing. Be as encouraging as you can during this period. Let him come up with a story, and maybe you can pitch in and offer ideas. Avoid the temptation of interjecting and guiding him on how he's supposed to do things. This creative interaction and support will help your child grow.

Another great way to engage him is by participating in household chores together as a team. It can be painting a room or putting away the groceries. Simple household activities are a great bonding idea. It also allows you to teach him problem-solving skills without depending on others. For instance, if a room needs to be painted, you can paint it together. Don't expect any perfection from him, but he would undoubtedly enjoy painting a wall; after all, it is a big canvas.

Sometimes, your child will seek your help or assistance with something he is doing. The answer might be simple, and you will be tempted to do it for him. Instead, step back and let him explore the different options available. You can also talk about the problem to prompt him to come up with suggestions and ideas. Allow him to implement these ideas and see for himself whether they work. If he cannot complete the task, you can step in and tell him what he can do. Don't complete the task for him but do let him implement your idea. If he comes up with some ideas and suggestions, offer praise and encouragement. However, do not go overboard with the praise, or he'll soon get used to excessive praise, which is problematic.

We live in a world dominated by devices. A simple way to encourage your child to explore his creativity is by teaching him photography. You can give him your smartphone or tablet and teach him how to click, save, and edit pictures. Once he gets the hang of it, set a time limit and let him explore the surroundings. If he takes any good pictures, tell him he did a fantastic job. You can also teach him how he can improve upon his photography skills.

Another way to encourage your child's creative thinking and imagination is by giving him a scenario and asking him to visualize how it will be. For instance, you can ask him what he would do if he were a character in his favorite cartoon or if he had superpowers. You can ask him, "What would you do if you were Superman for a day?" Patiently await his replies and prepare to be surprised. When you do this, don't ridicule his answers and ideas. Instead, join in and tell him what you would want to do.

Children love going out with their parents. The next time you visit the local museum or the zoo, talk to your child about it before the outing. Spend some time and tell him the different things he could experience there and expect to see. For instance, if you are going to the zoo over the weekend, tell him about different animals. When you go to the zoo, you can point out these animals and prompt him to recollect the different things you shared with him. This is also a great way to excite him about the outing.

Playing with water is fun. You can teach him how to make bubbles with a homemade soap solution. Children love bubbles! Give him a straw, show him how to blow bubbles, and start with your fun playtime. You can also teach him about light and rainbows using a garden hose. You need only to pick a date when the sun is shining bright in the sky. Go to the garden or the yard, pick up the garden hose, and put it on the mist setting. If you don't have a hose, you can use a spray can to spray in an area that catches direct sunlight. Once the natural light hits the stream of water or mist, a rainbow will be formed due to the refraction of light. He might be too young to understand what refraction means, but he will enjoy the rainbows he's making.

The next time it rains, let him play in the rain. Dress him up in his raincoat and boots, give him an umbrella, and let him have fun. It is okay if he gets dirty while stomping or rolling around in the mud. It is all right for him to enjoy spending time in nature. It will make him feel happy, and all the smiles and giggles will be worth cleaning up the mess.

Try cooking or baking together. If he loves chocolate chip cookies, try baking a batch along with him! Involve him in this activity, and he will love spending time with you. It also teaches him a little about cooking.

If there is a simple family problem, allow your child to come up with solutions for it. For instance, if the dining area is often dirty or at the living room is cluttered, ask him what can be done. It's not just the adults who can solve problems; even children can pitch in. For instance, if the question is, "What can we do about the messy living room?" He would probably say it needs to be cleaned regularly, or certain items need to be removed. If he gives you any suggestions, tell you to appreciate his inputs and see if it can be implemented. After he gives the suggestions, encourage him to help you implement them.

Another way to increase his creative thinking is by asking him simple questions. "What is the one toy you would want every child in the world to have?" Or "If you could get one gift every day, what would you want?" The idea is not to give him gifts or toys, but about letting him think about what he wants.

The next time you go grocery shopping, take your little one with you. Allow him to identify the different fruits, vegetables, and any other ingredients he knows. For instance, if his favorite fruit is an apple, allow him to pick up apples at the grocery store.

Go out for brief evening walks. Let him gather pebbles, rocks, twigs, flowers, etc., on his walks. Once you are home, you can sit together and make up a story about all the items you found. You can make a scrapbook and write about the different items he picked up. If he finds a shiny pebble, you both could conjure up a story it was left by an imaginary character!

Encourage your child to choose his clothes. It is a straightforward activity, but it prompts him to think about different colors, patterns, and combinations. If he puts together a new combination, ask him to wear it and ask him for his opinion. If he likes it, take a picture of it and put it in his room. If he doesn't like it, ask him what he would change about it.

If your child does something that makes him feel bad, don't tell him it doesn't matter. Instead, ask him why he is bothered by it, and how he can improve himself. By making him think independently, it increases his self-confidence. Once he identifies a reason and believes it is the right reason, praise him and congratulate his efforts.

While you follow all the tips discussed in this section, there are a few things you should never do – never interfere and don't take over. You can offer guidance, but that's all you're supposed to do. If your child is making a mistake, allow him to. Experience is an excellent teacher, and he will learn from his experiences. If your child does nothing to hurt himself physically, don't interfere. When you allow him to make his own decisions, it inspires a sense of confidence and independence.

Chapter Eight: Building Self-Esteem And Confidence

Most toddlers are inherently confident and surprisingly independent. As they grow and explore the world, their traits develop too. However, not all toddlers need to be confident and independent. Some can lie on the other end of the spectrum too. No two toddlers are the same. They all develop at their own pace. Don't be worried if your little one doesn't seem as confident as you would want him to be. There are different tips and strategies to develop his confidence levels. Yes, it is not just adults who could use a little help with these things; even toddlers need some assistance.

Self-esteem is how one sees his value in the world, while confidence is the belief in one's abilities to do things. These two concepts are interrelated. If your child is not confident, he might seem withdrawn, disinterested, and shy. The same behavior shows up if his self-esteem is a little low. The good news is you can help increase these two things in your little one. The sooner you start, the better it is. Here are tips that will come in handy.

Tips to Build Self-Confidence

Validation

It's a natural tendency to seek validation, and your toddler is no different. Therefore, be mindful that you validate his feelings and don't write them off. If he is a little shy, accept it, and validate his behavior. If you don't validate his feelings, you are prompting him to withdraw even further. When you talk about it, it allows you to talk about emotions and how he can handle them also. For instance, if you notice he is shy whenever he meets new people or goes to new places, acknowledge his feelings. You could say something like, "I understand you feel a little shy whenever we go to new places." After this, don't forget to reassure him it is okay to feel shy, but there are ways to deal with it. You could also tell him you feel shy at times, and how you deal with that.

No Labeling

Don't label your child as shy or nervous. Once you label him, the label itself becomes self-fulfilling. Also, these labels have a habit of sticking and making your child question and second-guess himself every step of the way. If you keep calling him shy, it's likely he will behave shyly. A better way to tell him this is by saying, "It is okay to feel shy." Instead of saying he is shy, you are sharing about a specific emotion.

Acknowledgment

If you notice your little one is doing something new or attempting something for the first time, don't forget to praise his efforts instead of concentrating on the results. If he realizes the effort counts, his willingness to make an effort increases. It also takes away the fear of failure. Yes, even children feel this. If you know that he often feels shy at new places, but he's willingly talking to someone, praise his effort. Tell him you appreciate what he's doing. Positive reinforcement is a great way to teach him what good behavior is. The praise he receives from you will act as an incentive.

Role Model

Since children learn by copying the behavior of those around them, it's time to start role-modeling good behavior. Show him how to be confident and resilient. Even when you feel unsure or frustrated because of something, stick to it, and ensure it reaches a logical conclusion. This is a great way of showing your little one how to be resilient. For instance, if you are frustrated with a project at work, don't give up. Instead, try to deal with it to the best of your abilities.

A Little Preparation

Low confidence can also stem from uncertainties about the future. Since the future is uncertain and you cannot predict it, the best way to remove this uncertainty is via preparation. If you are introducing him to a new activity, prepare him for it. Tell him about it, explain what's to be done, and show him the benefits it offers. For instance, if you need to take your toddler to a birthday party, tell him what he can expect. Once he knows what he can expect and the situation he will be in, he will be better equipped to deal with it.

Unconditional Love And Acceptance

Babies share a strong emotional attachment with their primary caregivers. This bond never goes away, and it doesn't weaken as they grow. They depend on you for love, safety, security, and support. If you show him he is loved and accepted unconditionally, the way he is with no terms or conditions; it instills confidence. It also shows he will be loved and appreciated regardless of whatever happens. Never underestimate the power of a genuine hug, a pat on the back, or even a kiss. It essentially conveys the feeling is that he is a worthy human, and he can be loved the way he is. If you show your love and acceptance only when he does something good, he will believe he needs to be perfect to attain such love and praise. Don't do this. Eventually, it creates undesirable behaviors and attitudes in the child – and more importantly, in the adult he grows into.

Encouragement

As with love and acceptance, even encouragement matters a lot. When you encourage your little one's ability to solve problems, it improves his self-confidence. Give him a few problems you know he can solve and allow him to solve them. Once he solves the problem, offer some praise and incentives. It could be something as simple as putting together a puzzle or learning a new game. If he does these things successfully, encourage him. Once he can complete things on his own, it instills a sense of confidence and independence.

Know Your Limits

Offering encouragement is important, and you should encourage him to deal with new situations in life. However, don't push him too hard. Similarly, you shouldn't be overprotective. Learn to be sensitive about how to encourage him and don't cross such limits. If it is something he isn't ready to do yet, don't force him. If you go overboard, you are encouraging him to withdraw himself even more. For instance, if you know he feels uncomfortable in new situations, don't send him to preschool without preparation. Instead, do these things slowly. When the change is gradual, his ability to adapt to it increases. Likewise, don't be overprotective and don't prevent him from trying out new things. Children tend to lack confidence when their parents are overprotective. If you keep doing everything for him, he will never learn how to be independent. The lack of independence will harm his confidence too.

Decision Time

By giving your toddler a chance to decide, you give him a chance to improve his confidence. It can be something as simple as deciding the clothes he wants to wear the food he wants to eat. Even if the clothes don't make sense together, let him decide. Once he sees how the clothes look on him, he might want to change his mind. When he knows he can decide for himself, it gives him a sense of control, which improves his confidence.

Ability To Say No

Allow your little one to say no. When he says no, learn to respect it. It doesn't mean you listen to him every time he says "no" to the different things you say. Instead, it merely means he should be allowed to a certain what he wants and doesn't want to do in certain situations. For instance, if your toddler fusses that he wants to wear sandals when it's cold outside, restrain yourself from saying no. Tell him, "You will feel cold if you wear your sandals today." After this, let him do it. While learning the consequences of his actions, he will become more confident. Create situations where "no" is a perfectly acceptable answer.

One Step At A Time

Whenever it comes to new situations, ensure that you split it into smaller steps for your little one while boosting his confidence. A major change can be scary for him. If he cannot get adjusted to such a change, it will hurt his confidence. Therefore, take things one step at a time. For instance, if he needs to start preschool, start slowly. You can visit the preschool, spend some time there, and maybe attend a class with him. Gradually, he will be comfortable on his own, and it isn't anything to worry about. Also, when he spends more time with kids his age, his confidence will improve.

Tips to Build Self-Esteem

One of the best gifts you can give your child is a positive sense of self. Self-esteem is also important if you want him to develop into a happy and productive individual. In this section, let's look at simple tips to enhance its overall sense of self.

In the earlier chapters, we talked about why it's important to give your child choices. Ensure the choices give are well within reason and acceptable alternatives to one another. When you give him choices and let him choose, it makes him feel empowered and in control. He also learns that he's in control of his actions *and subsequent consequences*. This is a great way to teach him how to make simple choices in life.

Never offer any insincere praise and unnecessary compliments. Praise your child's efforts when truly needed. Instead of concentrating on the results, praise him for his efforts. However, the praise should be genuine and necessary. For instance, don't gush that he is the next

Picasso when he paints something. Instead, you can say, "I appreciate your effort," or "You can be a god at it with a little practice." By doing this, you praise the effort that goes into the process, instead of offering insincere compliments.

Another great way to build self-esteem is by giving him age-appropriate responsibilities. Simple responsibilities for a toddler include putting his toys away, helping you arrange the dining table, or even selecting his clothes. You will learn more about different age-appropriate chores in the next chapter. When you give him some responsibilities around the house, it makes him feel like a valued and contributing member of the household. This simple feeling goes a long way in instilling self-esteem.

Restrain yourself from calling your child names, labeling him, or using sarcastic remarks to make a point. If he does something wrong, tell him what he did wasn't right, and show him how to do it properly. Don't call him any names or say things like, "This is stupid," or "How silly of you." Statements like this can sting and will slowly eat away at his self-esteem and confidence. You don't have to like everything your child does, but there is a proper way of showing your displeasure.

Most of us are guilty of drawing comparisons. Avoid comparing your child with those around him. If you keep comparing him with others, it will make him feel devalued, and you are essentially belittling him. He will question his self-worth, and it will erode his self-esteem and confidence. Remember, every child is different, and everyone grows at his own pace.

Ensure that you follow the advice in this section consciously and consistently. You cannot increase your child's self-esteem or confidence overnight. These personality traits are often a culmination of a variety of small events. Whenever your toddler completes a task or does something without being asked, it increases his sense of self-worth and confidence. A recurrence of such feelings over a period will enhance his overall sense of self-esteem, confidence, and independence.

Chapter Nine: Forming Positive Daily Habits

Habits aren't formed overnight. It is an ongoing process. If you keep doing a specific activity repeatedly at a given time, you develop a habit. The key to developing good habits is to start young. Work with your toddler and help him form good habits. An important aspect of doing this is to do it daily.

Positive Discipline for a Peaceful Home

Maintaining peace at home is quintessential for all family members. Constant power struggles and tantrums will disrupt this peace. The best way to reduce the risk of any unpleasantness at home is by establishing a routine for your little one. You will learn more about it in the subsequent sections. Now, let's look at simple ways to use positive discipline to create a happy and peaceful home environment.

Offer Information

Toddlers usually act out because it's the only way they know how to deal with the situation. They still don't know how to process, handle, and express themselves effectively. They are learning, and you need to be patient. A great way to speed up this process is by offering a lot of information to help them cope with the situation. If you notice your little one is acting out, provide information. Providing information isn't about questioning him, teaching him a lesson, or fixing the situation. It's merely just sharing things. For instance, if you notice your toddler is getting cranky because he cannot wear his nightclothes, tell him, "I realize you are getting frustrated that you cannot wear your pajamas properly." Or you might tell him, "I could help you, but you don't want me to. Why don't you try wearing them the other way and see?" By calmly providing information, you are offering him a choice. When you give him this information, you are essentially trying to understand his side of the story. Once he gets the information he needs, he'll be more pliable to listening to your direction.

Boundaries Matter

Boundaries matter a lot, and they are like safe walls that keep unnecessary things away from you. Remember, your toddler is still in the learning stage of understanding how to deal with frustration and boundaries. He is working on improving his confidence and self-control. If your toddler throws a tantrum or engages in a power struggle with you, it means you need to make more effort to teach him how to cope with the strong emotions he feels instead of doing away with your boundaries.

For instance, your toddler might throw a tantrum when you serve juice in a different sippy cup. Before every meal, give him two choices wherein he gets to choose the sippy cup he wants to drink from. Once he's chosen it, serve his beverage in that sippy cup. If he wants to change or use another sippy cup, tell him he needs to wait until the next meal is served. It teaches him patience and helps him deal with any frustration he feels. No matter what might have triggered the tantrum, step back and offer information.

Imagine the scenario. You splurge $ 300 on a new bag, go home, and realize it is not the bag you wanted, and now you wish to return it. However, the store has no return policy. It will make you feel frustrated and angry. These are the same things your toddler experiences when he feels powerless and helpless. By giving him choices and some information, you make him feel more in control.

Boundary Testing Is Common

Toddlers are curious, and a great way for them to learn is by testing the boundaries of those around them. If he's throwing a tantrum or is shouting, use every iota of self-control you must keep your calm. Losing your temper right now will not do either of you any favors. Instead of allowing your emotions to get the better of you, take control. Remember, the boundaries you have are your own. No one can invade them. Toddlers will test your boundaries. Just because he's testing your boundaries, it doesn't mean you give in. Stick to them without invalidating your child's emotions.

Physical Boundaries Matter Too

A lot of parents wrongly believe that physical boundaries cannot be used peacefully. Well, this is nothing more than a myth. If you realize your child will harm himself or someone around, it's okay to implement physical boundaries. For instance, if your toddler raises his hand to hit his sibling or another child, you can gently grab his arm to prevent him from hitting others. If you notice he's trying to climb on top of the kitchen counter, put your hand out to prevent him from doing this. Physical boundaries are important. If you see that your toddler repeatedly gets up from the bed after you tuck them in for the night, gently guide him back to the bed. These are simple examples, but they are effective and important to safety and health. This is so much better than indulging in any verbal power struggles with him. It's not only gentle, but it also doesn't undermine your little one's confidence. Try to keep it at a minimum, and always do it lovingly, peacefully, and gently.

Chores for Toddlers

The importance of creating a routine for toddlers has been repeatedly stressed in this book. A routine isn't just about encouraging him to wake up, brush, or sleep at specific times. Instead, it is about creating different tasks the toddler can do during the day. It is quintessential the tasks should be age-appropriate. For instance, expecting the toddler to do laundry or cut vegetables will merely set you and your tiny tot up for disappointment. While thinking about different chores your toddler can do, you merely need to simplify the regular chores adults do and make it age-appropriate. Since we are talking about creating a routine, the tasks you give him must become a part of his daily activities.

Once you make these tasks or chores a part of his routine, he will do them automatically, such as brushing his teeth. If your toddler refuses to do the task when you ask him to, you can try it together. Chances are your toddler will be excited to be assigned additional responsibilities around the house. After all, he sees his parents and other caregivers perform a variety of activities daily. Now that he has certain responsibilities, it will make him feel like an adult too. This is one thing that all children crave, regardless of their age; they all want to be treated as adults. By teaching him responsibilities, you show him that certain chores and tasks are a part of that responsibility.

In this section, let's look at some simple tasks to encourage your little one. Remember, you might have to teach him how the task should be performed a couple of times before he gets the hang of it. Before leaving it entirely up to him, do trial runs well; you both perform the tasks together. This is a great bonding technique too.

Tidying The Room

Encourage him to put his toys away after playtime. Show him how to put his toys away and ask him to repeat your actions. Fix a dedicated space for all his toys and encourage him to put them away in their designated spot. This simple task goes a long way while parenting and managing the household.

Putting Clothes Away

A simple chore you can get your little one involved in is putting his clothes away. Encourage him to put his dirty clothes in the laundry basket.

Cleaning Up After Meals

You can ask your toddler to carry his cup, bowl, plate, or even utensils to the dishwasher after a meal. He will probably hand them to you since he cannot reach the dishwasher.

Make The Bed

Another simple task you can give the toddler is to show him how to make his bed after waking up. He will not have the skills required to make stiff corners or fold the blanket, but he can help rearrange his soft toys and fluff the pillows. When you and your little one work together, it gives you a chance to teach him ideal behavior while strengthening the bond you share.

Putting Away Clean Laundry

After you fold the fresh and clean clothes, you can ask your toddler to help you carry them. You can give him a single item of clothing or two at the most. He need not place them in the dresser drawers, but he can help carry them there.

Putting Away Groceries

As soon as you get groceries home, ask your tiny tot for a little assistance. From washing vegetables to placing them in the refrigerator, these are little ways he can contribute.

Your toddler will be happy to tackle these chores with you. This is what big kids do, and you could excite him about doing these chores by telling him the same. While you give him a task, don't rush into it. Allow him to explore everything at his own pace. He is still learning the ways of the world. Whenever you notice he has completed the task, don't forget to praise him. If you catch him doing the task on his own with no reminder, offer praise. Don't go overboard with a preview offer, but don't be stingy with it either. When he knows he's doing something that you appreciate, it helps reinforce is positive behavior.

When you give him certain responsibilities around the home and give him the freedom to perform them as he sees fit, it helps increase his overall confidence levels. His self-esteem also increases. When his positive behavior is reinforced, his willingness to complete the tasks increases, he can take a while until he gets the hang of it. In the meanwhile, you need to be patient. Don't forget to teach him how to do the activity before assigning the responsibility. If he makes any mistakes, gently and lovingly correct him without chiding or shaming him. If he asks you about the activity, indulge him, and don't get irritated.

Besides the activities discussed in this section, there are several other chores where your toddler can participate. From removing weeds in the garden to dusting or mopping, setting up the table, wiping down the table, emptying the dishwasher, cleaning vegetables, and so on, there are many ways he can become an active member of the household. By encouraging him to actively participate in household activities, you are teaching him self-reliance and independence from a young age. These two traits go a long way in the real world, and it's a great way to ensure your toddler's overall development.

One simple thing you should never forget is *to manage your expectations.* Even if the task sounds simple to you, remember, you are dealing with a toddler. Learn to manage your expectations based on his abilities. For instance, he can help put his dirty clothes away in the laundry basket, but you cannot expect him to load the washing machine or fold his clothes. You can engage him while you do these things so he learns from your actions. Don't forget to appreciate his efforts; after all, he is trying his best.

Creating a Routine

Adults don't need a routine chart, but it would probably help us if we had one. When you have a specific routine, you know what's to be done at a point. Don't wonder, "What do I do now?" It equals putting your daily routine on autopilot. When you create a routine chart for your little one, it helps in the same way. After all, he is still learning, and to make things easier, use the chart.

It is also a great way to teach him how to manage his time and life in general. When you have a specific routine for your toddler, it allows him to experience different activities without excessive stimulation. If you constantly tell your toddler what he needs to do or should do, it can become frustrating for both of you. Instead, put all the tasks he needs to do in a chart form.

A common mistake many parents make is they forget that their primary responsibility towards their toddler is to make themselves obsolete. It might not sound pleasant, but you need to ensure that your child can take care of himself. When you give him certain responsibilities at home, it makes him feel independent. When he completes such activities, he will feel more confident. These feelings will stay with him throughout his life. However, it doesn't mean a routine chart is a silver bullet. Sometimes, he makes a mistake, and there will be resistance and lots of challenges along the way. However, it does provide a streamlined way of dealing with all these things without giving up.

The simplest way to avoid struggles in the morning or during bedtime is using this tool. Sit with your toddler and ask him all the things he needs to do before going to sleep. For instance, if his bedtime ritual includes a warm bath, changing into nightclothes, story time with his parents, singing a lullaby, and so on, make a note. Ask him what else he would like to add to all this. If he has any changes to make, consider his suggestions, and use them as helpful insights.

By allowing your toddler to be a part of this process, and creating his routine chart, he will feel more confident and capable. Instead of telling him what he needs to do next, you can point to this chart and ask him what he should be doing. For instance, before going to bed at night, a simple activity, you can ask him what clothes he wants to wear the following day. Once he chooses these clothes, it reduces the hassle of getting dressed in the morning. This comes in handy, especially if he goes to daycare or will be attending preschool.

Here is a simple example of a routine chart

- 7:30 AM-wake-up
- 8:00 AM- Potty and brushing
- 9:00 AM- Breakfast

In summary:

- Start creating a routine chart with your little one.
- Ask him what he would want to do and include these tasks in the charts.
- Whenever your little one accomplishes a task, take a picture of him doing it and place it next to the activity.
- Don't deviate from the routine charts, stick to them as much as you can.
- Don't add any unnecessary awards; focus only on completing the task.

There are no breaks when it comes to parenting, and parenting a toddler is a full-time responsibility. Use the hints provided to help you both and avoid any unpleasantness at home.

Chapter Ten: Growing Out Of Toddlerdom

Children grow up quickly. It might feel like it was only yesterday when you laid your eyes on your baby for the first time, and now, he is close to starting preschool. It can make one wonder where all the time went. Watching your child grow and develop is exciting and thrilling. However, change is seldom easy, but it can be handled effectively with a little planning and preparation.

Growing out of toddlerdom brings with it a variety of changes. The best thing you can do as your child's primary caregiver is to anticipate these changes and prepare yourself for it. Preparation helps eliminate uncertainty and anxiety associated with major life milestones, such as starting preschool. In this chapter, you will learn about the different tips you can follow to help you and your toddler prepare yourselves for the end of toddlerdom.

Preparing Your Toddler

Your toddler is learning and growing; change is an important part of this process. Don't just spring the idea of going to preschool on your toddler at the last instance. Instead, slowly prepare him for it. If you ensure that he is excited about this change, it becomes easier and more positive. Here are simple ideas you can use to increase his excitement and mentally condition him for the end of a toddler world.

If you and your toddler enjoy bedtime stories, include preschool stories. These days, there are different books available about preschool and choose one that appeals to you. You can sit together, read through the stories, or even choose an interactive storybook. Explain the story to him and ask how he feels about the character going to preschool. Ensure that you always maintain a positive attitude about it.

As mentioned in the previous chapter, toddlers are creative and imaginative. A simple way to get accustomed to going to preschool, while capitalizing on his creativity and imagination, is by playing pretend. You can use pretend play and encourage him to explore going to preschool. You can take turns pretending to be the child, parent, and teacher. From acting out a daily routine, such as waking up in the morning, having breakfast, going to preschool, and waving goodbye to reading stories, circle time, taking naps, and playing outside, there are different activities you can work on. It helps reassure your toddler that preschool does not differ that much from staying at home. The only difference is he gets to meet other kids. You can also warm him up to the idea of growing up by saying "big kids attend preschool." If he has any questions or worries about it, ensure that you carefully and patiently address all his concerns. You will learn more about this in the next sections.

Ensure that you take your child to his preschool and explore its surroundings before it starts. A tour of the preschool, playground, and different activities they conduct will prepare him for the actual upcoming events.

There are different small skills your toddler needs to perfect before going to preschool. Don't be worried if he doesn't get the hang of it yet, but he will once he goes there. Children are curious and learn better when they see others their age do the same things. A simple way to increase his self-help skills is by making a game of it. The simple skills you can teach him are putting on his backpack, unzipping his coat, trying on his shoes, and so on. For instance, create a competitive race. Use a stopwatch to check how long he takes to put on his shoes. If he needs to carry lunch or snacks to the preschool, get him used to eating from a lunch box. You can have a few "picnics" and pretend he is at preschool. This gives him a chance to open his lunchbox, unwrap his snacks, and so on.

If he is worried about missing his parents, sibling, or pets, you can give him a family photograph to take to preschool. He can also talk about his family with his peers and teachers.

Preparing Yourself

You have reached a major milestone if your child is starting preschool soon. There will be a variety of conflicting emotions running while through your mind. You will be excited about the fun your child will have, and the new journey he is setting out on. Simultaneously, it is also natural for parents to feel a little sad and anxious that their child is growing up. He was a tiny tot just a few months ago! All these emotions are common, and all parents experience them. However, with some preparation, the transition becomes easier.

Preparing your toddler for preschool is as important as preparing yourself. Yes, even parents need to prepare themselves emotionally and mentally for the moment of separation. Until now, you were probably used to spending all your time with your toddler. Now that he is nearing preschool, you need to get used to spending some time away from them. Perhaps the most difficult part of this is the first goodbye. Ensure that you maintain a positive and upbeat tone. If your child notices your apprehension, he will feel scared, too. Therefore, think of a special goodbye routine wherein you could kiss him on his palm and tell him to hold onto it all day long, or a special hug before he leaves. Ensure you resist the urge to go back into the preschool and rescue your toddler. This is an important step for him, and it is quintessential in his journey to adulthood. The first step matters a lot, and therefore, ensure that you are loving, kind, supportive, and compassionate to him.

To help with first-goodbye jitters and separation anxiety on his first day of the preschool, wait for a while after waving goodbye (about 15-20 minutes) to ensure that the transition becomes easy for your little one. You could also explore the classroom environment with your toddler to ensure that he is comfortable. *Usually, the parents struggle more than the toddler in accepting the change.*

Dealing with Worries

Starting preschool is a major change for your toddler, and he might have questions, concerns, or even worries about it. All these things are natural, and you should encourage open and honest discussions about it. There are two simple steps to address his worries and concerns. The first step is to listen to whatever your child has to say, and the second step is to notice any non-verbal messages he might be communicating

Being A Good Listener

Your child might not be able to articulate what he is feeling fully. However, that does not mean he has no worries. Whenever he starts talking to you about it, don't brush away his worries or write them off as silly. At the same time, don't jump into quickly and reassure him without even listening to what he has to say. It can be tempting to reassure him and soothe his worries but listening to him is also important. No matter how big or small his worries are, they are his concerns, and if you don't listen, it merely invalidates his feelings. If an adult listens to his concerns, especially one of his primary caregivers, it helps improve his self-esteem and confidence. Imagine how you would feel if someone wrote off your worries as silly.

When your child is talking about his worries is to be patient. If he has any worries or concerns when he starts preschool, it can influence his overall experience. To ensure he has the best possible experience, his mind should be free from worries. There could be some simple questions such as "Will my teacher be nice?" "Will I be able to make friends?" "What if I don't like it?" or "What if you forget to pick me up?" These worries might sound silly to an adult but are quite scary for your little one. Therefore, be a patient and compassionate listener.

Talk to him about the different feelings he might be experiencing. Tell him it is okay to feel happy, scared, excited, or even worried. Once you talk to him about these feelings, it will help ease his worries. Even adults feel better when we are told our worries are common, don't we? Talk to your child and tell him it is okay to feel a variety of emotions whenever we start something new. You can give examples from your life to make him more comfortable. Children often think adults don't experience feelings and emotions as they do. There might have been times when, as a child, you thought your parents, "Just don't get it." Well, times have changed, and the roles have reversed. You could share your own experiences. Even saying, "Honey, it is okay to be scared. Even mommy gets scared when she must do something new," can be helpful. If you have these conversations while following the tips mentioned in the previous sections, it will help make him feel more comfortable about going to preschool.

Being A Good Observer

Toddlers are talkative. Despite how much he talks, most 3-year-olds aren't good at explaining what they might be feeling or their worries. Therefore, watch his behavior. Kids act out whenever there's a major change involved and going to preschool is one such change. Different ways of acting out include withdrawing himself from his usual activities, excessive clinging, or aggressiveness. When children face a major lifestyle change, there can be a regression in certain areas. For instance, your little one might be potty trained, but if you notice he is having accidents, it is a sign of regression. It essentially means he is not coping well with a major change, and it is causing drastic changes in other established behaviors. If you notice he is constantly asking you to feed or clothe him, it's also a sign he isn't coping well. Parents can feel a little frustrated when they noticed their toddlers and aggressive behavior. You might also believe that if you keep helping him, he wouldn't do these things on his own or forget the desirable behaviors.

The best course of action is to simply let him go through this phase, and it will end. During this period, all that he needs is your support, unconditional love, encouragement, and lots of patience.

The concepts of positive discipline and parenting don't end once your toddler starts preschool. The basic techniques and tips discussed in this book can be used for parenting kids of all age groups. The only thing you need to change is the way you apply them. For instance, offering choices, information, communication of emotions, and understanding the kid's perspectives can be used whether you are parenting a toddler or a teenager. So, never stop using positive discipline, and you will be pleasantly surprised as you see your little one grow into a confident, self-assured, and independent adult with wonderful manners.

Conclusion

Now that you've gone through the different suggestions, tips, techniques, and strategies in this book, your idea of parenting will change. Learning about positive parenting and implementing positive discipline principles will help raise a child who is happy, confident, and well-adjusted to life. It also helps strengthen the bond you share with your little one. Your child might be the apple of your eyes, but sometimes, things get difficult. Parenthood isn't always about fun and games. You need to alternate between the roles of playing a good and a bad cop.

For children, their parents are not only their guardians and caretakers, but also their friends, mentors, and role models. Most things that kids learn are often from their parents. Therefore, playing the role of a parent is important and crucial in your child's development. By setting a good example, you are encouraging your toddler to follow. Dealing with a child doesn't mean you have to raise your voice or dole out punishments. Instead, it's about communicating with your child and avoid certain behaviors by making him realize the difference between good and bad behaviors.

Discipline is one area a lot of parents struggle with. If you face any guilt in this aspect, cut yourself some slack. Loving your child means disciplining him, too. Discipline is the simplest way to ensure he does nothing that puts him in harm's way. From learning about dealing with tantrums to fixing any misbehavior and building self-esteem and confidence, positive discipline comes in handy.

In this book, you were introduced to simple tips and techniques you can follow to successfully potty train your toddler. If bedtime seems like an uphill battle, and every night makes you feel drained out and tired, try either of the sleep training tactics discussed in this book. Besides this, there is one simple rule you must always remember- positive parenting starts at you and with you. The sooner you start, the better it is to use these tactics for parenting your little one.

Now that you are armed with all the information you need, the next step is to implement the simple strategies, suggestions, and tips in this book. Remember, parenting is an ongoing process. It takes a lot of patience, consistency, effort, dedication, and unconditional love. Once all these elements are in place, sprinkle them with positive discipline and voila- you can raise your toddler to be a happy, well-adjusted, and confident child.

Resources

10 Positive Parenting Solutions to Deal with Toddler Tantrums. (2017, July 31). Kids Club Child Care Centres website: https://www.kidsclubchildcare.com.au/parenting-solutions-for-toddler-tempers/

Advice for Sleep Training Your Toddler. (n.d.). Happiest Baby website: https://www.happiestbaby.com/blogs/toddler/toddler-sleep-training

Barakat, I. (2017, March 10). Positive Discipline and Child Guidance | Living Montessori. Living Montessori Education Community website: https://www.livingmontessori.com/positive-discipline-and-child-guidance/

Bellefonds, C. (2018, December 4). Nightmare or Night Terror? What to Expect website: https://www.whattoexpect.com/toddler/sleep/toddler-nightmares-night-terrors/

Bilich, K. (n.d.). 12 Common Potty-Training Problems. Parents website: https://www.parents.com/toddlers-preschoolers/potty-training/problems/12-common-potty-training-problems/

Bhandarkar, S. (2013, November 18). Positive Discipline 101: How to Discipline a Child in a Way That Actually Works. A Fine

Parent website: https://afineparent.com/be-positive/positive-discipline.html

Brill, A. (2017, November 17). How to correct a child's 'bad' behavior with positive parenting. Motherly website: https://www.mother.ly/child/practicing-positive-discipline-with-your-kids-is-not-only-possible-its-powerful

Eisenberg, N., Zhou, Q., Spinrad, T. L., Valiente, C., Fabes, R. A., & Liew, J. (2005). Relations among positive parenting, children's effortful control, and externalizing problems: a three-wave longitudinal study. Child Development, 76(5), 1055–1071. https://doi.org/10.1111/j.1467-8624.2005.00897.x

Gagne, C. (2019, November 2). How to stop co-sleeping: An age-by-age guide. www.todaysparent.com website: https://www.todaysparent.com/family/family-health/how-to-stop-co-sleeping-an-age-by-age-guide/

Godfrey, D. (2019, July 25). Bedtime Without Struggling. Positive Parenting website: https://www.positiveparenting.com/bedtime-without-struggling/

How to correct a child's 'bad' behavior with positive parenting. (2017, November 17). Retrieved from Motherly website: https://www.mother.ly/child/practicing-positive-discipline-with-your-kids-is-not-only-possible-its-powerful

How to Potty Train: The Guide to Positive Potty Practices. (n.d.). www.kindercare.com website: https://www.kindercare.com/content-hub/articles/2015/january/toilet-training-the-guide-to-positive-potty-practices

Jones, A. (2019, June 21). 12 Positive Parenting Techniques To Make Potty Training A Peaceful Event. Romper website: https://www.romper.com/p/12-positive-parenting-techniques-for-potty-training-according-to-experts-18020415

Li, P. (2016, December 17). Positive Parenting - 8 Tips to Discipline The Happy Way. Parenting For Brain website: https://www.parentingforbrain.com/what-is-positive-parenting/

MONTESSORI AT HOME: Positive Discipline Examples & What To Do [YouTube Video]. (2019). https://www.youtube.com/watch?v=SckUevGH-Pk

Neppl, T. K., Conger, R. D., Scaramella, L. V., & Ontai, L. L. (2009). Intergenerational continuity in parenting behavior: mediating pathways and child effects. Developmental psychology, 45(5), 1241–1256. https://doi.org/10.1037/a0014850

Novak, S. (2018, June 27). Potty Training Tips. What to Expect website: https://www.whattoexpect.com/toddler/potty-training/how-to-start-potty-training/

Phillips, R. (n.d.). Toddlers 101: Understanding Toddler Development. Parents website: https://www.parents.com/toddlers-preschoolers/development/behavioral/toddlers-101-understanding-toddler-development/

Tantrums at All Ages: What is normal? (2020, February 19). Positive Parenting Solutions website: https://www.positiveparentingsolutions.com/parenting/tantrums-at-all-ages

Toddlers and Challenging Behavior: Why They Do It and How to Respond. (2019). ZERO TO THREE website: https://www.zerotothree.org/resources/326-toddlers-and-challenging-behavior-why-they-do-it-and-how-to-respond

Tired Mom Supermom - Providing Support On Positive Parenting. (n.d.). Tired Mom Supermom website: https://tiredmomsupermom.com/

Toddler Development. (2019). Medlineplus.gov website: https://medlineplus.gov/toddlerdevelopment.html

CPSIA information can be obtained
at www.ICGtesting.com
Printed in the USA
LVHW080052130121
676292LV00041B/14